Classic Cooking

with

®

By Elizabeth Candler Graham

Great-great-granddaughter of the founder of Coca-Cola®

and Ralph Roberts

HH Hambleton-Hill Publishing, Inc. • Nashville, Tennessee

Published by Hambleton-Hill Publishing, Inc.
Nashville, Tennessee 37218

Printed and bound in the United States of America

ISBN 1-57102-500-6

Edited by Pat Hutchison
Interior design and electronic page assembly by WorldComm®
Photographs on back cover: Elizabeth by Evelyn Graham, Ralph by Angelika K. Shore

Library of Congress Card Catalog Number: 94-78607

10 9 8 7 6 5

The authors and publisher have made every effort in the preparation of this book to ensure the accuracy of the information. However, the information in this book is sold without warranty, either express or implied. Neither the authors nor Hambleton-Hill Publishing, Inc. will be liable for any damages caused or alleged to be caused directly, indirectly, incidentally, or consequentially by the recipes or any other information in this book.

The opinions expressed in this book are solely those of the authors and are not necessarily those of Hambleton-Hill Publishing, Inc.

Trademarks

Coca-Cola®, Coke®, the Dynamic Ribbon Device, and the design of the contour bottle are registered trademarks of The Coca-Cola Company, as are **Sprite**®, **Fresca**®, **Minute Maid**®, **Mello Yello**®, **TAB**®, **cherry Coke**®, **diet Coke**®, and **Coca-Cola classic**®. Names of other products mentioned in this book that are known to be or are suspected of being trademarks or service marks are capitalized. Use of a product or service name in this book should not be regarded as affecting the validity of any trademark or service mark.

CONTENTS

1 INTRODUCTION 3

2 MEATS 23

5 MAIN DISHES 73

6 VEGETABLES 83

7 SOUPS 93

8 SALADS   101

9 BREADS   107

10 FRUITS   113

11 DESSERTS 123

12 CANDIES 163

13 BEVERAGES 167

14 MICROWAVE 183

15 MISCELLANEOUS 187

PREFACE

The concept of **Classic Cooking with Coca-Cola**® arose after accidentally stumbling across several recipes using **Coca-Cola**. We tried them, and they were delicious! So after a lot of work and research, we offer you this wonderful collection of tasty, tempting recipes using **Coca-Cola** and other products of The Coca-Cola Company.

Asa G. Candler, a hardworking Georgia Methodist in the pharmaceutical trade, acquired the formula for **Coca-Cola** some one hundred years ago for a paltry $2300. Dabbling with the formula, changing it by choice and at the insistence of the federal government, Candler parlayed his modest investment into what has become one of the world's most successful companies.

Great-great-grandfather Asa passed control of the company on to his sons and daughter, who in turn sold control in 1919. The Candlers' fascination with **Coca-Cola** has continued to this day, and many of us are still stockholders. And, of course, we serve nothing but **Coca-Cola** in our homes.

We have watched with pleasure the incredible growth and success of The Coca-Cola Company, not only in the United States, but throughout the world. Yes, **Coca-Cola** is in good hands, and we can look forward to the pleasure of drinking and cooking with our favorite beverage for many years to come.

Elizabeth Candler Graham

Elizabeth Candler Graham

Acknowledgements

Classic Cooking with *Coca-Cola*® actually started out as a quest to track down a few family photographs to complete a scrapbook project. But after finding so many wonderful recipes using **Coca-Cola** products, we just had to pass them along.

This book would not have been possible without the tremendous help and encouragement of many people. We have amassed an incredible amount of information about **Coca-Cola** and my family, the Candlers. Not only was the Candler clan enthusiastic, but the kind people connected with The Coca-Cola Company and Emory University were also happy to participate. We are grateful for all of their assistance.

In researching the story of **Coca-Cola** and the Candler clan, most of my interviews included fond memories and stories about all of the wonderful meals that the family shared over the years. Like all Southerners, generations of Candlers have taken great pride in being able to "set a good table" and provide delicious and interesting dishes to share with family and friends. In fact, so many of our discussions centered around food, that one would almost think that for generations all we've done is sip **Coca-Cola** and plan another big meal!

A special thanks is due to all of my friends and relatives who have shared their memories and their recipes.

To Ralph Roberts, not only for his valuable assistance as coauthor, but also for his continued enthusiasm.

To my good friend Pat Hutchison, who spent many long hours typing in and then verifying recipes. Pat's research makes this cookbook the wonderful compilation that it is.

To Kathryn Hall and Tammy Best, who worked long and hard on this book.

To those fantastic people at our distributor, Associated Publishers Group in Nashville, and especially to Van Hill, Sandra Hall, Donetta Krantz, Robert Komisar, Julia Hoover, Sally Hertz, Cary Kretchmar, Jay Woodruff, Jan Floyd, Gwen Watts, Andy Tolbird, and all the other excellent people whose magnificent efforts in sales made this book a success from the first!

Thank you all!

The famous artist and illustrator N. C. Wyeth (father of Andrew Wyeth) did the painting for this gorgeous 1936 fiftieth anniversary advertisement of **Coca-Cola**. (Courtesy of The Coca-Cola Company)

Classic Cooking

with

®

METRIC CONVERSIONS

1/8 teaspoon = 0.5 ml
1/4 teaspoon = 1 ml
1/2 teaspoon = 2 ml
1 teaspoon = 5 ml
1 tablespoon = 3 teaspoons = 15 ml
1/8 cup = 1 fluid ounce = 30 ml
1/4 cup = 2 fluid ounces = 60 ml
1/3 cup = 3 fluid ounces = 90 ml
1/2 cup = 4 fluid ounces = 120 ml
2/3 cup = 5 fluid ounces = 150 ml

3/4 cup = 6 fluid ounces = 180 ml
1 cup = 8 fluid ounces = 240 ml
2 cups = 1 pint = 480 ml
2 pints = 1 liter
1 quart = 1 liter
1/2 inch = 1.25 centimeters
1 inch = 2.5 centimeters
1 ounce = 30 grams
1 pound = 0.5 kilogram

Baking Dish Sizes

American	Metric
8-inch round baking dish	20-centimeter dish
9-inch round baking dish	23-centimeter dish
11 x 7 x 2-inch baking dish	28 x 18 x 4-centimeter dish
12 x 8 x 2-inch baking dish	30 x 19 x 5-centimeter dish
9 x 5 x 3-inch baking dish	23 x 13 x 6-centimeter dish
1 1/2-quart casserole	1.5-liter casserole
2-quart casserole	2-liter casserole

Oven Temperatures

Fahrenheit Setting	Celsius Setting
250°F	120°C
275°F	140°C
300°F	150°C
325°F	160°C
350°F	180°C
375°F	190°C
400°F	200°C
425°F	220°C
450°F	230°C

CHAPTER 1

INTRODUCTION

In the process of researching the history of **Coca-Cola** and the Candler family, we kept running across recipes using **Coca-Cola** as an ingredient. We tried a few of these recipes and found them to be delicious! So after some munching and crunching, the idea of doing a cookbook finally occurred to us. We then began searching for and collecting recipes using **Coca-Cola**.

It's amazing what we found! We'll tell you about it in this chapter, and we'll give you some information about the various sweetening agents in The Coca-Cola Company's wonderful products. We'll also tell you some interesting anecdotes about the history of the company, its founding family (the Candlers), and some of the other people who have made **Coca-Cola** what it is today—one of the greatest marketing successes in all of history.

Cooking with Coke®

The idea of enhancing the flavor of food with **Coca-Cola** is by no means a new one, thus the very appropriate use of the word classic in the title. From its introduction in the 1880s, there is no doubt that someone has been using **Coca-Cola** for cooking.

Coca-Cola was first made in Atlanta, in the American South. We Southerners have always been greatly concerned about food and drink. In fact, some of the most delicious dishes you'll ever taste come from south of the Mason-Dixon line. So is it any surprise that this traditional Southern preoccupation with drink and food quickly resulted in the combining of the two? It surely shouldn't be.

The popularity of **Coke** quickly spread out of Atlanta, through the South, and then through the nation. So it was no wonder that people, both rich and poor, began cooking with **Coca-Cola**, creating **Coca-Cola** based desserts, and using it in all sorts of other tasty and delightful ways. And today, just as the popularity of **Coca-Cola** as a refreshing drink has spread across the world, so too has the use of **Coca-Cola** as an ingredient in cooking.

We'll be absolutely honest and frank with you here. When the concept of doing **Classic Cooking with** *Coca-Cola*® first popped into our brains, we said, "Yeah, it's a great idea, but we would be lucky to find twenty or thirty recipes using **Coke**—if that many."

So after some discussion back-and-forth, we decided we could put out an honest book if we used those twenty or thirty recipes and leavened them with Candler family recipes and other traditional Southern recipes. In other words, use **Coca-Cola** as the basis for an otherwise conventional Southern cookbook, of which there are already some six zillion on the market.

As the research progressed, we found to our pleasant surprise that in the over one hundred years of its existence, **Coca-Cola** has inspired a lot of recipes. So instead of just a few, we found literally hundreds of recipes using **Coca-Cola** or other products of The Coca-Cola Company. In fact, we found ourselves with too many recipes and were forced to leave out some of the lesser ones. We did not have to pad the book at all—every single recipe in this book uses **Coca-Cola** or another product of The Coca-Cola Company.

Why cook with **Coca-Cola**? Because it's traditional, and because the foods prepared from the recipes that follow are just plain good!

Where We Got the Recipes

This book is the largest collection of recipes using **Coca-Cola** ever gathered in one place—a long and time consuming task, but an accomplishment of which we are mighty proud. We hope that you will enjoy many delicious meals as a result of our loving efforts.

But we cannot claim to be the first **Coca-Cola** cookbook—that honor belongs to The Coca-Cola Company itself. *When You Entertain, What To Do, and How* by Ida Bailey Allen was copyrighted in 1932 by The Coca-Cola Company (Atlanta, Georgia) and dedicated to "The Pause that Refreshes in the Home." Untold thousands of this book were distributed, but if you can find a copy today, it is a rare and valuable collectible.

As an interesting sidelight, Ida Bailey Allen (1885-1973) deserves the title "Queen of Cookbooks." Her cookbooks were published from 1920 through 1982 and covered an incredible range of recipes. In addition to the book for **Coca-Cola** in 1932, she compiled books on Canada Dry Ginger Ale and several other products. She also garnered notable achievements in writing more conventional cookbooks. We proudly salute her and follow in her pioneering footsteps.

We started our search for recipes using **Coca-Cola** at the logical places, the Archives of The Coca-Cola Company and the libraries of Emory University—both in Atlanta. The latter place is significant because both the Candlers, who founded The Coca-Cola Company, and the family of Robert Woodruff, who led the company so gloriously for many decades, have donated their private papers and books to the University. Both families have libraries and collections named for them. There is an incredible wealth of information about **Coca-Cola** and the families behind our favorite beverage at Emory, and the people there were very kind to us during our research. Again, we thank them and our wonderful friends at The Coca-Cola Company as well.

After that we haunted used book shops and antique malls, buying every old cookbook we could find that had recipes using **Coca-Cola** (a surprising number). The number of recipes began to swell, as did we in taste-testing those wonderful foods.

Still the number of recipes was not enough. Because **Coca-Cola** is now sold worldwide, we decided to broaden our search. We revved up our computers and roared out onto what is soon to become the information superhighway, the Internet. The Internet allowed us to access libraries all over the world. More importantly, we made friends with those wonderful fans of **Coca-Cola** on the **alt.foods.cocacola** news group.

Our cyberspace call for recipes using **Coca-Cola** resulted in a lot of great ones. Jane Elkins in North Sidney, Australia, was especially helpful, sending us a treasure-trove of recipes via electronic mail from her computer to ours. Jane sent us some great chicken recipes and one for pot roast that's simply grand.

Over this worldwide computer network, Tomer Strolicht in Richmond Hill, Ontario, Canada, added a whole new dimension to cooking with **Coca-Cola**—wild game. His mouth-watering recipe for saucy venison with **Coca-Cola** is in Chapter 2 on page 60. Many responded to our call, and all those who sent us a new recipe first will receive free autographed copies of this book.

So that's basically how we collected these recipes—by research in Atlanta, from old cookbooks, and from up and down the information highway of the Internet. Oh, and from one other source, us! We took a number of traditional Southern recipes and did a little experimentation, substituting **Coke** or other products of The Coca-Cola Company for various ingredients such as water. Those that tasted really good are in this book. Some of our failures even the dog wouldn't eat, so they went into the bottom of the garbage can.

NutraSweet®

We expect a few people will complain about how few recipes we have using **diet Coke** or other low calorie products such as **Fresca**. The problem is cooking with NutraSweet, and it's one we need to discuss here. NutraSweet is about the best thing to come along since sliced bread. It is the sweetening agent in **diet Coke**, **Fresca**, and a lot of other low calorie products, but using it in the cooking process, as it turns out, can be a real no-no.

According to the nice people at NutraSweet itself, NutraSweet breaks down and looses its sweetness under prolonged heat. While you can cook with NutraSweet, it's not recommended if the sweetener is exposed to heat. What you can do, suggest the people at NutraSweet, is add the product after the heating process is over. They also say that they are working to make NutraSweet stand up to heat, but that it may be a while yet. You might try substituting **diet Coke** for the **Coke** in the recipes in this book that do not involve heat. We assume that this will work okay. As for any recipe where heat is applied, you are on your own. The NutraSweet company was firm in telling us not to recommend the use of their product for cooking, so we don't.

Sugar

One more thing about sweeteners that you should be aware of concerns **Coca-Cola** itself. All of the traditional recipes, of course, were developed using the original formula of **Coca-Cola**. Sugar was the traditional sweetener in original **Coke** for almost 100 years, until "Black Tuesday" (as Coke fans call it), or April 23, 1985. That's when The Coca-Cola Company introduced "new" **Coke**, a reformulation of the traditional product. A mighty uproar from all over the United States of disgusted **Coke** fans shook Atlanta to its roots. The Coca-Cola Company responded (some say narrowly averting a lynching) by reintroducing the original formula as **Cola-Cola classic.**

The taste is more or less the same, but the sweetener assuredly is not. In the United States, **Coca-Cola classic** uses (as it says on the can) "high fructose corn syrup or sucrose" as its sweetening agents. Not having any of the old pre-Black Tuesday **Coke** with sugar to use in testing, we can't tell you how much (if any) difference this change in sweeteners makes in the recipes. Perhaps none, because the traditional recipes still tasted mighty good to us.

If you are a purist and want to use **Coca-Cola** with sugar instead of high fructose corn syrup, there are a few ways of getting it! **Coca-Cola** bottlers in countries other than the United States are more likely to be using real sugar still. People on the Internet tell us that **Coca-Cola** from Canada, Mexico, and the Bahamas is made with sugar. If you have friends in or traveling to those countries, you might be able to import some "sugar" **Coca-Cola**. There are rumors that some **Coca-Cola** bottling companies in the United States still use sugar, but we were unable to confirm this (corn syrup is cheaper). If you know of any, please let us know.

Also, around the Jewish observance of Passover, some bottlers in the United States occasionally put out "Passover **Coke**," since some Jewish people (those of Ashkenazi extraction) are not allowed to consume corn products at this time. Check kosher delicatessens for this kind of **Coke.**

Coca-Cola® Syrup

The **Coke** you buy at drugstore soda fountains and so forth is made from **Coca-Cola** syrup to which is added carbonated water. This syrup is a wonderful ingredient for cooking, if you can get it.

All **Coca-Cola** bottling companies, of course, sell syrup to their wholesale customers—drugstores, restaurants, fast-food outlets, theaters, stadiums, and other businesses serving fountain-type drinks. Unless you own or work at one of these businesses, or a friend does, it will probably be hard to get **Coca-Cola** syrup from a bottler. They are not too keen on selling to individuals since the wholesale quantities they sell are usually far more than individuals want.

Your local drugstore may be the answer. Many pharmacists still buy **Coca-Cola** syrup in gallon or half-gallon containers. It is sometimes prescribed for vomiting or nausea. They will often sell you small quantities of syrup without a prescription for cooking purposes.

It's great, by the way, just poured directly on ice-cream.

Dr. Jack R. Jones of Jonesboro, Arkansas, tells a story about this latter use of the syrup. When he was a student at Auburn University in the early 1940s, he worked as a soda jerk in a drugstore. The meal that was all the rage at that time was a foot-long hot dog, a frozen root beer, and a **Coke** "sundie" (spelled that way instead of *sundae*). The **Coke** sundie consisted of two scoops of rich vanilla ice cream with **Coke** syrup poured over it. Dr. Jones made hundreds of these for customers. It was (and our publisher says "Still is!") great!

A Brief History of Coca-Cola®

Coca-Cola has become a universal product. You don't need to speak the language. Ask for a **Coke** on the sands of the Mideast, the pampas of Argentina, among the lush foliage of a Polynesian island, or under the "Red Rising Star of the East" flag in China, and you'll get a **Coke**!

For a century now, millions of soda fountain clerks and machines have mixed one ounce of **Coca-Cola** syrup with six-and-a-half ounces of carbonated water, and millions upon millions of people have plunked down their nickels, pesetas, francs, rupees, and rials for the pause that refreshes.

Coca-Cola has become a billion-dollar business, but it all started quite modestly on a May day in 1886, behind the house of one John S. Pemberton of Atlanta, Georgia.

Pemberton was a druggist who, like so many others of the day, dubbed himself "Doctor," although no evidence of a formal medical degree has ever been found. He had fought with Pemberton's Calvary and served as a captain with General Joe Wheeler during the War for Southern Independence. At the end of the war, Pemberton, like the rest of his fellow Georgians, was working hard to rebuild his life in the defeated Confederacy.

For four years, Pemberton stayed in his hometown of Columbus, Georgia, but by 1869, the aggressive vibrancy of rebuilding enticed him northward to Atlanta. There he set up business as a druggist and pharmaceutical chemist. By 1870, he had joined with other businessmen to form Pemberton, Wilson, Taylor and Company. Pemberton was an idea man, a creative wizard more at home mixing up amazing panaceas to cure the ills of humanity than he was with profit and loss statements and ledger books. It would always be others who reaped the rewards of his creations, but that never stopped him from trying.

During the next fifteen years, Pemberton went through several business affiliations, the major one being the company of Pemberton, Iverson and Dennison. In 1885, he established the J. S. Pemberton Company and, not long afterwards, the Pemberton Chemical Company. By that time many of his medicines were quite well-known across the South. They included Extract of Styllinger (a medicine for the blood), Gingerine, Globe of Flower Cough Syrup, Indian Queen Hair Dye, and Triplex Liver Pills. Those were the booming days of patent medicines and snake-oil salesmen, before the Federal Food and Drug Administration came along to insist on testing and truth. As long as the paying public could be made to believe that a product cured insomnia, grew hair, loosened the bowels, and silenced mothers-in-law, all was fair in the free market.

Somewhere in this concocting of liver pills and hair dye, Pemberton came up with the idea for a new tonic. The actual moment and method of the creation of Pemberton's Tonic, as it was appropriately first called, has been clouded, colored, and flavored by legend and word-of-mouth retellings, with elaborations and embellishments added as each teller saw fit. In later years, generations of publicity and advertising people further reworked and polished the legend for the sake of the bottom line.

E. J. Kahn, Jr., in his book *The Big Drink*, writes that the syrup for Pemberton's Tonic was based on Pemberton's French Wine Coca, which was patented in 1886 and sold as "an ideal nerve and tonic stimulant." Kahn states that Pemberton had simply taken out the wine, substituted "a pinch of caffeine," and added a few ingredients including extract of cola and other oils. It is believed that Pemberton was trying to create a cure for headaches.

What is known for sure is that on or just before May 8, 1886, in the backyard of 107 Marietta Street, Pemberton cooked up the first batch of syrup for his new tonic in a brass kettle. Then later on that Saturday he took a jug of his syrup down to Jacobs' Pharmacy, one of Atlanta's leading soda fountains. The fountain, with its elaborate counter running for twenty-five feet along one entire side of the drugstore, was leased and managed by Willis E. Venable.

Pemberton talked Venable into mixing some of the syrup with water and trying it. The soda fountain man liked the taste and agreed on the spot to sell it. So it was on that day, in May, that someone first paid his or her nickel for a glass of Pemberton's concoction and drank it there in the store.

According to Cecil Munsey, author of *The Illustrated Guide to the Collectibles of Coca-Cola*®, it was decided at about this point that with Venable having signed on to market the tonic, a new name was needed. Within a few days, the name "Coca-Cola Elixer and Syrup" was chosen. Involved in the naming process were various members of Pemberton's company—Pemberton himself; his business partner, Edward W. Holland; David D. Doe; and company secretary and book-keeper, Frank M. Robinson.

It was Robinson who hit upon the idea of putting together the words "coca" and "cola," two of the tonic's ingredients. He liked their alliterative, easy-to-remember sound. He also suggested that the name be written in the Spencerian script that was a popular form of penmanship at that time. It was from his pen that the neat and precise *Coca-Cola* signature originated. Pemberton and the others were pleased with Robertson's ideas except for the length of the name. The words "Elixer and Syrup" were dropped, and the product became known simply as "Coca-Cola," as it still is today.

Later that month on May 29, 1886, the *Atlanta Daily Journal* had the honor of carrying the first advertisement for **Coca-Cola**. It was a simple ad, with "**Coca-Cola**" printed in plain type instead of script. The ad stated: "**Coca-Cola**, Delicious! Refreshing! Exhilarating! Invigorating! The New and Popular Soda Fountain Drink, containing the properties of the wonderful coca plant and the famous cola nuts. For sale by Willis Venable and Nunnally & Rawson."

As indicated by the reference to "Nunnally & Rawson," in less than a month after its introduction, more than one establishment was serving Coca-Cola. Of course, it wasn't the Coke we know today. It was flat. There was no carbonation, no fizz.

As the unconfirmed story goes, this was changed accidentally on the morning of November 15, 1886. A certain gentleman by the name of John G. Wilkes had partaken heavily of bottled spirits the previous night. Awakening with a splitting headache, he sought relief from a nearby pharmacy. Since **Coca-Cola** had been created and touted by Pemberton to be, among other things, a cure for headaches, it was no surprise that someone wanting quick relief would try it. Wilkes desperately seated himself at the soda fountain and called, no doubt softly and carefully while holding his shattering skull together, for a glass of **Coca-Cola**. The soda fountain clerk mixed the **Coca-Cola** syrup with carbonated water by mistake. The fizzing result was pleasing to Wilkes and brought relief to his pounding temples. Whether or not this story is true, it soon became the standard practice to mix **Coca-Cola** syrup with carbonated water.

Coca-Cola, however, was not an astounding sales success under Pemberton's management. In its first year, only 25 gallons of syrup were sold, that being enough for about 3,200 glasses. Approximately $50 was realized in sales, but $73.96 had been spent on advertising. The next year, 1887, sales rose dramatically to more than one thousand gallons. Although Pemberton was rightly convinced that he had a winner, he was in failing health and didn't have the capital to properly advertise and promote the product.

In July 1887, Pemberton offered his friend George S. Lowndes twothirds interest in the **Coca-Cola** formula if Lowndes would invest in the company. While Lowndes found the offer attractive, he was not interested in actually going out and selling jugs of syrup himself. He went to someone with sales experience, Willis Venable, to see if he wanted in on the deal as well. Venable did. However, there was a problem. Venable did not have the money for his share of the purchase. Lowndes offered to lend it to him.

The resulting deal with Pemberton was a payment of twelve hundred dollars for two-thirds interest, with Venable promising to reimburse Lowndes for six hundred dollars from **Coca-Cola** sales profits. In the papers that were signed on July 8, 1887, the twelve hundred dollars was described as a loan to Pemberton with repayment to come from his share of the profits. On July 15, a modified contract was signed, changing the deal to read that Pemberton's loan was to be repaid from total profits.

Another stipulation of the deal was that the new partners were to take over ownership of all the items and fixtures used in the manufacture of **Coca-Cola** by "paying the said Pemberton therefor [sic] the original cost." In an inventory drawn up on July 27, 1887, this cost was computed to be $283.39. These assets—including advertising materials such as posters and signs—were loaded in a wagon and moved to Jacobs' Pharmacy. According to a later president of The Coca-Cola

Company, although not listed in the inventory, a brass kettle, sixty tin cans, and a percolator also made their way over to Jacobs' Pharmacy.

After the inventory was in place, Willis Venable took over the manufacturing of **Coca-Cola** in between the already time-consuming task of running his soda fountain. George Lowndes was not pleased with the result. Orders for syrup often piled up because Venable was too busy to make it. Lowndes bought out Venable on December 14, 1887, and then quickly sold the two-thirds of the company to Woolfolk Walker, salesman for the Pemberton Chemical Company, and Walker's sister, Mrs. M. C. Dozier. The purchase price was twelve hundred dollars, Lowndes' original investment.

Walker, over the next few months, realized that he could not make the company really profitable without working capital to expand facilities and to advertise properly. He sought help from two men. One was Joseph Jacobs, who owned Jacobs' Pharmacy and on whose premises the equipment to manufacture **Coca-Cola** syrup was still set up. The other was a very successful druggist Walker had met while selling for Pemberton. That man was Asa Griggs Candler.

The three men joined in a new firm called Walker, Candler and Company. On April 14, 1888, they purchased Pemberton's remaining one-third of the rights to **Coca-Cola** for the sum of $550. Although on paper the new company bought out Pemberton, it was actually Candler who put up the money with the understanding that he would own the third. This gave Walker and his sister two-thirds interest in **Coca-Cola** and Candler the other third. Then on April 17, Candler purchased another third from Walker and his sister, giving him two-thirds of the company.

Pemberton, in all, received $1200 plus $550 plus the $283.39 for equipment and other inventory, or a total of $2,033.39 for the creation of **Coca-Cola**. Sadly he did not even live long enough to enjoy that amount. His health continued to worsen rapidly, and he died some four months later on August 16, 1888. To honor their late associate, Asa G. Candler, as chairman of the association of the Atlanta druggists, called for all drugstores in the city to be closed during Pemberton's funeral, as they were.

Later that same month on August 30, 1888, Asa Candler bought the remaining ownership of **Coca-Cola** from Woolfolk Walker and his sister for one thousand dollars. Candler had now spent a total of twenty-three hundred dollars to obtain full and complete rights to **Coca-Cola**. Asa G. Candler had already built his pharmaceutical business into one of the most successful in the South by seeing and seizing opportunities. **Coca-Cola**, from his vantage point, had possibilities. But after discovering the product, Candler decided that Pemberton and the other people involved in producing and selling it were not doing a very good job. Candler didn't want to be part of some slipshod, poorly managed operation. He wanted total control of **Coca-Cola** so that he could maximize its potential. He was a sharp and canny businessman with the skills and confidence to go after what he wanted.

Candler was intentionally secretive in the way he handled the purchase of **Coca-Cola**. He was one of the leading pharmacists in Atlanta and was assumed to have a lot of money. Had Pemberton known that Candler was behind the buy offer, in all likelihood, the price would have gone up. Candler was also very clever in spreading the risk among other partners until the profit-making potential was obvious. Only then did he go for full ownership and control.

There is little question that **Coca-Cola** would not exist today if Asa Candler had not become involved with it. Neither Pemberton, Lowndes, Willis Venable, nor Walker and his sister had the marketing skills or the capital to achieve more than selling a few hundred gallons of syrup a year to local soda fountains. **Coca-Cola** was, frankly, not that special when compared to the better-established competition such as Moxie. The true genius of Asa Candler was marketing, which turned this patent medicine from a mere tonic into a soft drink that automatically gets put on grocery lists. He was to become the "Father of **Coca-Cola**." But in 1888, all this was still to come.

One might wonder what Candler saw in this little known tonic that had sold barely a thousand gallons in its not quite two years of existence. And while Candler was a clear-eyed businessman, the answer lay not so much in what he saw, but what he felt—constant, horrific migraine headaches.

Asa had lived with these headaches since suffering a terrible accident as a child. His mother, Martha Bernetta Beall Candler, described the mishap in a letter to his oldest sister, Florence Candler Harris, dated December 11, 1862.

> My dear daughter I know you are uneasy that you dont hear from us I waited some time to hear from you but mail quit coming. The Confederate government has taken the contract and now we will get the mail when it is convenient for them to send it. We are all well except Asa. He fell out of a loaded wagon and the wheel ran over his head just above the ears and crushed his head and left him very badly but stronger today. He is now we think out of danger. In his fever he says he wants to see you. The first word he said was when is my sissie coming?

> I shall never see my dear sister Harris any more. Jessie has nursed him day and night without number. Though he can eat & set up he cant hear. The nerves of his left eye were crushed so that he cant see or hear on that side but he can whistle yet. His escape from death is a miricle and only by the thoughtful kindness of God was he saved, for which I most humbly and cincerly give him all the honor & praise & cincer thanks.

One of Pemberton's goals in formulating **Coca-Cola** was to present a cure for headaches. During most of the first decade of its existence, **Coca-Cola** was considered to be a medicine. Candler himself advertised it in the 1890s as "The Wonderful Nerve and Brain Tonic and Remarkable Therapeutic Agent."

Candler confirmed his belief in **Coca-Cola** as a headache tonic in an April 10, 1888, letter to his brother Warren, who was living in Nashville and would later become an influential Methodist bishop.

> You know how I suffer with headaches. Well, some days ago a friend suggested that I try **Coca-Cola**. I did & was relieved. Some days later I again tried & was again relieved. I determined to find out about it. Investigation showed that it was owned by parties unable to put it fairly before the public. I determined to put money into it & a better influence. I put $500 of the first and am putting a goodly portion of what I have of the last. . .

Asa was already thinking of expanding **Coca-Cola**'s market. "Now I don't want to make a merchant or peddler out of you," Asa went on in his letter to Warren, "but if you could either send me the name of a party who wants to engage to introduce **Coca-Cola** into Nashville (the best soda fountain town in the South I am told) I will make it interesting to him. It is a fine thing—certainly."

What Asa had in mind was a classic promotional ploy. He would supply two gallons of syrup free—enough for 256 servings when mixed with carbonated water—if the druggist would send him the names of 128 men and women. Asa then would send a ticket to the druggist's fountain to these people, entitling them to a free glass of **Coca-Cola**. Once they tried a glass, Asa was sure they would want more. The druggist then would have 128 servings left to sell.

It was an interesting and amusing facet of Asa's personality that he would conscript his brother, a Methodist preacher, into selling his new product. Later he would have another brother, a judge, drinking

Coca-Cola and thus giving it at least tacit endorsement. Asa Candler used any and all resources to sell his product, family included. Everybody in his family worked for **Coca-Cola**, even if they were not on the payroll. In the case of Warren, a good preacher had to be able to sell the word of God—selling **Coca-Cola** should have been, at least in Asa's mind, a snap compared to that.

Brother Warren did help, as is evidenced by a letter Asa sent him on June 2, 1888. In it, he thanks Warren for his assistance with a Mr. Walker. He reports that Walker sold thirty gallons in Nashville, although he had expected him to sell one hundred. Asa wrote that they were doing "modestly well with **Coca-Cola**. Its only obstacle is that Pemberton is continually offering a very poor article at a less price & the public who pays for **Coca-Cola** & are not fulfilled commensurably decide that it is a fraud."

It would seem that Pemberton's company—if not Pemberton himself—was still marketing something similar to the **Coca-Cola** formula which, of course, would have still been known to them. At least they would have known the version that Pemberton had sold to what became Candler's company.

Asa Candler's great-granddaughter, Nancy, remembers her grandfather, Asa G. Candler, Jr. (called Buddie by the family), and others in the family talking about the senior Asa's headaches and about the original formula.

"Buddie always said that he and [his brother] Howard were sent over to Haverty's Hardware to buy something to mix the ingredients up in. Aunt Florence said that Asa, Sr., changed the Pemberton formula several times to make it taste better and to increase its shelf life. Asa believed **Coca-Cola** had terrific qualities as a medical cure-all. He had migraines and the **Coca-Cola** helped ease his headaches."

For several years after gaining control of **Coca-Cola**, Asa Candler continued to sell it more as a medicine than as a refreshing drink. In writing to a doctor in Cartersville, Georgia, on April 2, 1890, Candler extolled its therapeutic qualities.

> We desire to call your attention to the Ideal Brain Tonic, **Coca-Cola**, a delightful summer and winter soda fountain beverage which has proved to be very beneficial and agreeable in hot or cold weather at all times of the year to those who desire a tonic stimulant . . .
>
> The medical properties of the Coca Plant and the extract of the celebrated African Cola Nut, make it a medical preparation of great value, which the best physicians unhesitatingly

endorse. and recommend for mental and physical exhaustion, headache, tired feeling, mental depression, etc.

Coca-Cola has such a very marked effect in refreshing and reviving the drooping spirits and taking away the tired feeling and so promptly relieves the headache, that it is constantly making good friends, who not only use it themselves but gladly recommend it to others.

Candler got into the **Coca-Cola** business primarily because he saw a chance to make a profit. He stayed in it because it became so profitable that he was eventually able to drop all the rest of his pharmaceutical business. However, he was first attracted to this new **Coca-Cola** because it cured his headaches. Candler continued to believe strongly in the medicinal properties of the drink for the rest of his life, even though for various reasons, including the insistence of the federal government, he would change the original formulation.

Frank M. Robinson came up with the name "**Coca-Cola**" because Pemberton's tonic contained extracts of both the coca leaf and kola nut. The coca leaf has no relation to and should not be confused with the cacao seeds from which come the cocoa beverage and chocolate.

Kola nuts—which are really seeds of an African tree rather than nuts—contain the stimulant caffeine. There is no question that caffeine was in the original formula of **Coca-Cola** and still is—except for the caffeine-free versions, of course. The big question is: Were the coca leaves used in **Coca-Cola** "de-cocainized?" The answer is yes and has been for many decades.

What else is in **Coca-Cola**?

Well, that's a *secret,* and one that is better protected than any of the Pentagon's. A mystique has arisen over the past century about the **Coca-Cola** formula. Only a relatively few people have ever been allowed to participate in the actual mixing of **Coca-Cola**, and, of those, most only put in ingredients by number, such as so much of No. 4, so much of No. 5, and so on. They did not know what these substances actually were, especially not that most secret of ingredients, *7X.*

The magic formula, jealously guarded as it is, has added a great deal of romance to **Coca-Cola** over the years. There has been much speculation about its various components, and competitors have spent untold amounts trying to duplicate it. The original and still secret formula for making **Coca-Cola** rests in an "unobtrusive" safety deposit box at the Trust Company of Georgia in Atlanta. As a collectible, it is worth a few thousand dollars perhaps, but to The Coca-Cola Company it has been and continues to be worth literally billions of dollars!

Fortune magazine (in a famous July 1931 article) went to some lengths to determine and expose the magic formula. *Fortune* was one of the respected but sometimes brash publications of Henry Robinson Luce, who also founded *Time* and *Life*. Taking on something as big as **Coca-Cola** was exactly the indomitable Mr. Luce's cup of . . . well, in this case, of **Coca-Cola**.

The article contended first that **Coca-Cola** was ninety-nine percent sugar and water. The other one percent, it said, was made up of caramel; fruit flavors (including lavender, fluid extract of guarana, lime juice, and various citrus oils); phosphoric acid; caffeine from tea, coffee, or chocolate; "Merchandise No. 5," which was three parts de-cocainized coca leaves and one part kola nut; and a secret ingredient known only as *7X*.

It is true that **Coca-Cola**, at least as it was made in the past, had a lot of water and sugar. In a standard "batch" of 5,000 gallons of syrup, there were *28,000 pounds of sugar!* But then no one ever said **Coke** was not fattening. Today sweeteners other than sugar are used.

Many others have speculated and attempted to duplicate the immensely valuable **Coca-Cola** formula and still do. Various "outsider" chemists doing analysis of **Coca-Cola** have claimed detection of ingredients such as cinnamon, nutmeg, vanilla, and glycerin.

How close have they been to the true formula? Well, among other things, the *Fortune* article left out the vanilla—Asa Candler preferred the Madagascar variety. We have no intention of revealing the full formula here—it is, after all, the proprietary property of The Coca-Cola Company, and its attorneys have teeth that are both big and sharp in such cases. Yet when the Candler family sold the controlling interest in the company in the early 1920s, certain family members kept copies of the formula—or at least of the one in use at that time. This, knowing the Candlers as we know those wonderful Candlers, was probably an insurance policy of sorts—just in case the Woodruffs failed to make a go of it and the rights to the formula reverted to the family. And we would not be surprised if that's not the reason there are still a few copies of the formula squirreled away in safety deposit boxes, although by now it is pretty obvious that the new owners of **Coca-Cola** have done rather well for themselves over the last seventy years. Be that as it may, we have talked to people who actually have the fabled secret formula.

It is something of a paradox in this age of heightened consumer awareness that millions of Americans blithely drink can upon can and bottle upon bottle of a beverage filled with unidentified ingredients. And further, if you quite reasonably asked the company what it contained, you would only get the answer, "It's a secret!" And if you persisted and did manage to find out in some way, they would sue you if you revealed the formula.

The Coca-Cola Company will continue fighting to keep their valuable and highly proprietary formula a secret. However, in recent years, consumer pressure has caused the federal government to require stricter and stricter listing of ingredients on food products. Take a can of **Coca-Cola classic** today and look at the small vertical print on its side. You will find The Coca-Cola Company reluctantly revealing that this drink contains:

> Carbonated water, high fructose corn syrup and/or sucrose, caramel color, phosphoric acid, natural flavors, caffeine.

The words "natural flavors" mean a lot. These include the "coca" and the "cola," and all the other ingredients that really make the product what it is. Among these ingredients is that most secret of substances, 7X. The Coca-Cola Company and other companies making food and beverage products with proprietary formulas have battled for decades against totally divulging their component parts—so far they continue to win. Buy any candy bar and the wrapper tells you exactly what is in it, but not so that delicious and refreshing soft drink.

What is the most secret of secret ingredients, the holy 7X?

Many of Asa Candler's grandchildren and great-grandchildren had been told as kids that **Coca-Cola** did contain cocoa. They all liked chocolate and cocoa and attributed the good taste of **Coca-Cola** to that ingredient. Could it be that cocoa is the famous "secret ingredient" of **Coca-Cola**? One person telling this story was Asa Candler's daughter, Lucy, who most likely did know the formula.

We, of course, can neither confirm nor deny this.

In the 1920s and 1930s, under the leadership of the legendary Robert Woodruff, The Coca-Cola Company expanded rapidly and surely into the industry leader that it remains today.

Atlanta was excited about this new era of The Coca-Cola Company. Everybody wanted a piece of the company—after all, it had made millions for Asa Candler, why not them? This was the entrée for many a bright young man with his eye on the future to not only establish a terrific career with a young, growing company, but to also be introduced into high society circles. This influx of eligible young men was certainly a boon to young ladies in Atlanta at that time. High society circles expanded to include these young **Coca-Cola** employees, franchisees, and their families.

Coca-Cola bottling franchises cost little to set up (about five thousand dollars in the early days) and produced great cash profits. Generally, once an operation was running, the owner would set up members of his family in similar operations. When you started up your **Coca-Cola** bottling franchise, your family automatically became a part of the family of **Coca-Cola**. For generations to come, these people and their families would produce and sell **Coca-Cola** and laugh all the way to the bank. The people who owned bottling franchises quickly became some of the wealthiest people in town and rapidly rose to positions of prominence in the civic and business circles.

Even during the Great Depression of the 1930s, The Coca-Cola Company continued to increase its profits. In 1928, for the first time ever, sales of bottled **Coca-Cola** surpassed sales of **Coca-Cola** from soda fountains. And on July 27, 1929, an ad in the *Saturday Evening Post* featured the first use of the slogan "The pause that refreshes."

As America entered the dark days of the early thirties, the phrase "Buddy, can you spare a dime?" was a constant refrain. A dime, back then, would buy two glasses of **Coke** and quite often did. People got a little lift from the dire realities of Depression times by sipping an ice-cold **Coke**. Almost everyone could come up with the occasional nickel, so the company kept growing.

In 1930, as the Depression deepened, The Coca-Cola Company had record sales of $34,580,493, almost half of which (more than $13 million) was profit. In 1935, the first **Coca-Cola** coin-vending machines were set up. In 1937, automatic fountain dispensers were introduced, finally insuring consistency in **Coke** served over the counter. Also in this era, the six-pack of **Coca-Cola** was first offered and proved to be a popular success.

Coolers were also designed and provided at a very low cost to retailers by the company. Today everyone is familiar with soft drink coolers in stores with the prominent advertising logos on their sides. Back then, however, it was a new and innovative idea which brought **Coca-Cola** out from behind the counter and made it highly visible.

And, of course, there were the constant advertising campaigns. The main thrust of advertising during the many Woodruff years was to equate **Coca-Cola** with American life. In that, the company's advertising has quite undeniably succeeded in a most emphatic way. **Coca-Cola** has slowly shifted from a Southern icon to an American icon. We are **Coke** and **Coke** is us, and so the world perceives us.

The evolution of ad slogans is interesting. In the early twenties, there was "Enjoy Thirst," then came "Pause and Refresh Yourself," a theme that was to be repeated for years. Other slogans of the era were: "Refreshment Time," "Around the Corner from Anywhere," "Continuous Quality," "With a drink so good, 'tis folly to be thirsty," "Stop at the Red Sign," "A Hot Day Made Cool," "It Had to Be Good to Get Where It Is," and "7 Million a Day," the latter referring to the number of servings of **Coke** sold every day.

As more and more profits were pumped into the advertising campaigns of the 1920s, slogans included "The Shortest Distance Between Thirst and Refreshment" and "The Best-Served Drink in the World." Finally, in 1929, came the classic "The Pause that Refreshes."

By the time the Depression had ended and World War II began, The Coca-Cola Company was several times the size it had been under Asa Candler and was selling millions of dollars of **Coca-Cola** every year.

That growth has continued to the present. Today, The Coca-Cola Company consistently leads the soft drink industry in sales. Our favorite drink, we can be assured, is going to be around for a long time to come!

FOREVER!

Ralph's Bonus Recipe

As a little boy, growing up in the South in the 1950s, one of our special treats was to take a cold **Coca-Cola** and pour a bag of salted peanuts inside. The taste sensation of simultaneously drinking the **Coke** and eating the peanuts is indescribably delicious. I tried it again just today. It's as great as I remembered!

Ralph Roberts

RECIPES

Notes to the Reader

When the recipe calls for **Coca-Cola**, it refers of course to **Coca-Cola classic**.

Measures vary. If a recipe specifies something vague like "1 can of shrimp" (without giving a size or weight in ounces), it's the cook's choice as to how much is put in. So on these traditional recipes—while we tested with a specific amount—we intentionally did not put that amount in the recipe, leaving it as close to the original as possible. Season and add ingredients to your taste.

Tastes and cooking skills vary. We say we think all the recipes in this book work reasonably well. We don't say you'll like them all (although we hope you will). In other words, we make no guarantees as to what kind of results you'll get—that would be impossible given the myriad of tastes people possess and the availability of ingredients.

Because these recipes came from many sources and span a century, they reflect different cooking styles which have been in vogue at various times. For example, the old-fashioned barbecued chicken (page 38) calls for greasing the rack and the pan and using a lot of shortening. Several recipes call for monosodium glutamate. The current understanding of healthy cooking frowns on these practices, but they were valid in their era. We have retained the spirit of the original recipes, but you may want to alter some of these practices as you cook.

We don't guarantee you won't gain weight either. Some of these recipes are mighty rich and delicious. This is not a diet book and was never meant to be.

In other words, we don't guarantee anything at all, but we certainly hope that you will enjoy this book.

Please feel free to send your comments to:
Elizabeth & Ralph
Hambleton-Hill Publishing, Inc.
1501 County Hospital Road
Nashville, TN 37218

CHAPTER 2

MEATS

S o that you won't think classic cooking with **Coca-Cola®** is just desserts, drinks, and other such sweet puff and fluff, we start out by getting right to the *meat* of the matter. Prepare to be made hungry!

Coca-Cola® goes just as well on meats as it does when drunk with these delicious and satisfying dishes. A longtime Southern tradition has been a wonderfully simple barbecue sauce consisting of 1/2 cup catsup to every cup of **Coke®**. Place this mixture on the meat as it cooks, or simmer it and serve as a condiment on the side. Chicken, beef, turkey, pork, and fish are all delightfully enhanced by this quick sauce you can whip up in mere seconds!

We begin with the sauces and move on.

SAUCES

Quick Barbecue Sauce

> 1/2 cup catsup
> 1 cup **Coca-Cola®**

Simply mix together and pour on meat as it cooks. A really delicious and easy sauce!

Super Meat Sauce

4 slices bacon, diced
3 ounces butter or good olive oil
1 medium size Spanish or red onion, chopped
5 fresh mushrooms, chopped
4 cloves garlic, chopped
8 ounces ground pork (lean shoulder or other part)
8 ounces ground lean chuck
8 ounces **Sprite®**
1-1/2 pound can tomato puree
4 ounce can tomato paste
1/2 gallon whole tomatoes (#5 can)
1 quart chicken or beef stock (or tomato juice)
1/2 cup chopped parsley
1 stalk celery, chopped
2 bay leaves
pinch of thyme leaves
pinch of rosemary leaves
pinch of oregano
pinch of grated nutmeg
1 clove
a few leaves of fresh basil or salt and pepper
parsley, for garnish

In a saucepan, cook the bacon. Add the butter or oil and onions. When lightly browned, add the mushrooms and garlic, then the pork and beef. After a few minutes add the **Sprite®** and then the rest of spices (except the parsley), tomatoes and liquids.

Cook slowly for about 2 hours. Before serving, remove the clove and add the chopped parsley. Garnish with additional parsley.

Orange Sauce
(for Ham, Chicken or Turkey)

1 tablespoon cornstarch
1 cup **Minute Maid®** orange juice
1/4 teaspoon salt
1/4 teaspoon cinnamon
1/4 cup sugar

2 teaspoons grated orange peel
1 teaspoon angostura bitters
1 orange thinly sliced
additional grated peel for garnish

Mix the first seven ingredients and cook over low heat until clear. Pour the sauce over meat.

Garnish with orange slices and additional peel.

Meat Marinade and Gravy

1 cup **Coca-Cola®**
1 cup cooking oil
1 tablespoon A-1 sauce
1 clove garlic, crushed
2 tablespoons Worcestershire sauce
2 teaspoons soy sauce
1 can mushrooms

Combine all of the ingredients. Marinate meat at room temperature for 2 hours before cooking. Use this same marinade to baste a roast—very often. Cook at 300 degrees. Use a meat thermometer for desired doneness.

Serve with mushroom gravy (use remaining marinade—add mushrooms and thickening.)

Super Barbecue Sauce

1 cup **Coca-Cola®**
2 cups Worcestershire sauce
1-1/4 cups tomato catsup
1/4 pound butter
1 tablespoon salt
4 teaspoons sugar
1 to 2 tablespoons freshly ground black pepper

Combine all of the ingredients in a heavy pot or kettle and bring to a boil over low heat. Cook, stirring frequently, at least 30 minutes. Brush on foods as they are grilled.

©1978 The Coca Cola Company

For over 100 years now, **Coca-Cola**® has been advertised as going well with food. Which, indeed, it does, as shown on this recipe card for baked ham issued by The Coca-Cola Company in 1978 (part of a set). It should come as no surprise to anyone that hungry Southerners from the 1890s on used **Coke**® as a food ingredient in addition to drinking it as a refreshing beverage. Many of the recipes in this book are decades old, part of this great tradition of **Coke** *in* food as well as **Coke** with food!

CHICKEN

Chicken in Coca-Cola® Sauce

This is the Candlers' answer to France's *Coq au Vin*. If you enjoy experimentation, **Coke®** deliciously replaces wine in many other recipes also.

> 3 1/2 to 4 lb. chicken, cut up (approximately 8 pieces)
> salt and pepper to taste
> 2 tablespoons olive oil
> 2 tablespoons butter or margarine
> 1 lb fresh mushrooms (cut up if large)
> 1/4 cup chopped spring onions
> 2-3 cloves garlic, diced very fine
> 4-5 tablespoons flour
> 2 cups **Coca-Cola®**
> 3/4 cup chicken broth
> 4 sprigs of fresh parsley
> 1 bay leaf
> 1/2 teaspoon rosemary

Dry chicken with paper towels. Season with salt and pepper. Heat the oil and butter in very large cast iron skillet. Add the chicken pieces and cook until golden on one side. Then turn and cook the other side until golden. Chicken will have to be cooked in batches. Place on separate plate and set aside.

In the same pan, add mushrooms. Cook over medium heat until golden. Add onion and garlic and cook, stirring until softened. Sprinkle flour into pan, and cook, while stirring, until a light color (1-2 minutes). Add **Coca-Cola®**, broth, and herbs. Stir to blend. Cook for 4-5 minutes. Return the chicken pieces to the pan.* Bring to a boil, cover and simmer gently for 25-30 minutes or until tender.

(* If skillet is too small for entire mixture. Pour sauce into large cooking pot (4-6 quart) and bring to a boil. Then add the chicken pieces to the pot. Cover, reduce heat to simmer and cook as above.)

Remove chicken from pot, arrange on platter. Skim fat. Discard bay leaf and pour sauce over the chicken. Serves 4.

Braised Chicken Wings

3/4 cup **Coca-Cola®**
1/4 cup soy sauce
2 tablespoons brown sugar
1 teaspoon dry mustard
2 green onions, cut in 1 inch pieces
10 chicken wings, separated at joints

In a medium saucepan, combine all the ingredients. Cover and heat to boiling, then reduce heat and simmer 30 minutes. Uncover and simmer 15 minutes longer, basting frequently.

Serve hot or cold.

Coq au Coke®

2 small broilers cut in half, lengthwise
1/4 cup unsweetened pineapple juice
1/4 teaspoon nutmeg
1 stick butter
1/2 cup **Coca-Cola®**

Salt the chicken and let it stand for 1 hour, then pan broil gently in butter until lightly browned and reserve the drippings. Place the chicken in a baking dish or electric skillet. Add the pineapple juice, **Coca-Cola®**, and nutmeg. Cover and simmer for 30 minutes at 300 degrees turning occasionally. (Add water, if necessary). For gravy, remove the chicken and add the juice from the skillet drippings, simmer and dilute with water to the desired consistency.

Boneless Wonder

Here's a wonderful recipe that sounds disgusting from the ingredients listed but tastes wonderful.

1 lb flank steak or chicken breast
    or whatever boneless meat you like
12 ounces **Coca-Cola®**
1 tablespoon coffee

1 1/2 teaspoon tomato paste
1 large onion cut up
1 medium clove garlic
1 tbsp ground cumin seed
oil for frying

Cut meat into bite sized pieces. Heat oil in wok or frying pan. Add meat, cook until browned. Add onions and garlic, cook until onions are soft. Add tomato paste and stir until everything is coated nicely. Add coffee and stir until dark shiny brown color develops. Pour in **Coke®** and add cumin seeds. Cover and simmer ten minutes.

Tastes great over rice or pasta.

Barbecued Chicken with Crust

2 1/2 lb fryer, disjointed
4 cups Corn Flakes, crushed
1/3 cup **Coca-Cola®**
2/3 cup catsup

Mix **Coke®** and catsup. Dip chicken in the sauce and roll in Corn Flakes until well coated. Line a shallow baking pan with aluminum foil. Place chicken in pan skin side up.

Bake at 350 degrees for 1 1/2 hours.

Barbecued Chicken

2/3 stick butter or margarine
1 small onion
1 cup catsup
1 **Coca-Cola®** (12-ounce)
1 chicken, cut up
salt and pepper, to taste

Sprinkle salt and pepper on the chicken pieces and set them aside. In a large skillet, melt the butter and add the onion, catsup and **Coke®**.

Add the chicken and cook on low heat for approximately an hour, keeping covered.

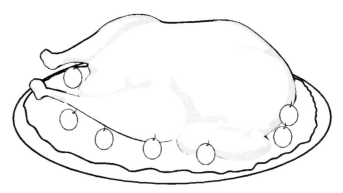

Chicken Wings Over Atlanta

3 pounds chicken wings
1 cup soy sauce
3/4 cup brown sugar
1/2 cup margarine
1 teaspoon dry mustard
3/4 cup **Sprite®**

Place the chicken in a shallow baking dish. In a saucepan, combine the remaining ingredients and cook until hot. Cool the sauce and pour it over the chicken. Marinate for 2 hours, turning occasionally. Leave the chicken in the sauce and put it in a 350 degree oven; bake for 45 minutes, turning once. Spoon the sauce over the chicken while baking. Remove the meat from the sauce and broil it on both sides until browned.

Company Chicken

2-1/2 to 3 pound fryer, cut into 6 to 8 pieces
salt and pepper, to taste
10-3/4 ounce can cream of chicken soup
10-3/4 ounce can cream of celery soup
10-3/4 ounce can cream of mushroom soup
1/2 cup **Sprite®**
1/2 cup slivered almonds
1/4 cup grated parmesan cheese

Wash and pat dry the chicken pieces. Place the chicken pieces in a greased casserole dish and sprinkle with salt and pepper. Pour the remaining ingredients over the chicken in the order given. Bake at 350 degrees for 1 to 1-1/2 hours, depending on your oven.

This is very good served over rice or noodles. For a change of taste, add curry and serve with raisins, coconut, chutney and other appropriate condiments.

Hawaiian Chicken

    3 pound broiler-fryer chicken, cut up or favorite parts
    3 tablespoons oil
    1 large onion, chopped
    14 ounces catsup
    14 ounces **Coca-Cola®**
    2 tablespoons white vinegar
    1/3 cup brown sugar
    2 tablespoons soy sauce
    20 ounce can pineapple chunks, drained

In a saucepan, saute the onion in hot oil until golden brown. Add the catsup, **Coca-Cola®**, vinegar, and brown sugar and heat until the sugar dissolves. Put the chicken pieces in a greased casserole dish and pour the sauce over it. Sprinkle with soy sauce. Bake, uncovered, at 325 degrees for 1 hour and 15 minutes.

Baste every 10 minutes. Add the pineapple chunks and bake 15 minutes longer.

Chicken and Mushrooms

5 tablespoons butter
3 ounce can mushrooms
flour
salt and pepper to taste
4 chicken breasts, halved
2/3 cup **Coca-Cola®**
sliced Swiss cheese

In a skillet, melt 2 tablespoons of butter, stir in the drained mushrooms and cook for 5 minutes over low heat. Remove the mushrooms from the skillet. Lightly flour, salt, and pepper the chicken breasts. Add the remaining butter to the skillet and brown the chicken. Remove the chicken from the skillet and add the **Coca-Cola®** and bring it to a boil while scraping the bottom and sides of the pan. Stir the mushrooms in and remove from heat. Place the chicken breasts, skin side down, in a casserole dish. Pour the **Coca-Cola®** and mushrooms over and bake uncovered for 35 minutes in 350 degree oven. Turn the chicken over, and spoon the mushrooms on top. Cover with thin slices of cheese. Bake 15 minutes longer, basting frequently.

Indonesian Chicken

8 halves chicken breasts
1/2 cup oil
1 small onion, chopped
1-1/2 pound can tomatoes, mashed
salt and pepper
1 cup chicken bouillon
1/2 cup **Coca-Cola®**
1/2 teaspoon salt
1/2 teaspoon paprika
1 tablespoon parsley, chopped
2 rounded tablespoons cornstarch

In a large skillet, heat the oil and brown the chicken. Add the onion, tomatoes, salt and pepper. Cover and simmer 1 hour. Remove the chicken, and place it skin side up on serving dish. In a bowl, mix the bouillon, **Coca-Cola®**, salt, paprika, and parsley together and add to the skillet containing the tomatoes and onion. Bring the mixture to a slow boil. Thicken with cornstarch and boil, stirring, about 5 minutes. Pour the sauce over the chicken. Serve this on a bed of rice and sprinkle with a few green peas for color. Side dishes of grated coconut, fried Chinese noodles and chopped peanuts can accompany this, to be sprinkled over each portion as it is served.

Cantonese Boneless Fried Chicken

> 3 tablespoons soy sauce
> 1/2 teaspoon sugar
> 12 drops ginger syrup
> 3 deboned chicken breasts
> 1 cup flour
> 2 tablespoons cornstarch
> 1 egg
> 3/4 cup **Sprite**®

In a bowl, mix together the soy sauce, sugar and ginger syrup. Brush this mixture on all surfaces of the chicken and let the pieces stand for 1 hour. In a bowl combine the flour, cornstarch, egg and **Sprite**® and beat the mixture until it has the consistency of a smooth, thin batter. Coat the chicken pieces thoroughly with the batter and fry in deep fat or oil at 375 degrees until tender and golden brown.

Rolled Chicken Breast

> 8 chicken breasts, deboned
> 1/2 teaspoon fresh parsley, chopped
> 1 small clove of garlic, pressed
> flour
> 1-1/2 teaspoons butter
> salt and pepper
> 8 bouillon cubes
> 7 or 8 cups water
> 3/4 cup **Coca-Cola**®

Roll the chicken in parsley and garlic, sprinkle with salt and pepper and coat with flour. In a skillet, brown the chicken in butter. Place the chicken in a baking dish. In a bowl, dissolve the bouillon cubes in water and combine with the **Coca-Cola**®. Pour this mixture over the chicken. Bake uncovered for 2 hours at 350 degrees.

Tarragon Chicken

6 small chicken breasts
4 blades of fresh tarragon
2 tablespoons butter
6 small white onions, sliced thin
1 cup sour cream
1/2 cup **Coca-Cola®**
1/2 cup rich chicken broth
salt
pepper
nutmeg
rice

Prepare the rich chicken broth by cooking 2 cups of chicken broth over a high heat until it is reduced to 1/2 cup and set aside. In a skillet, cook the chicken breasts lightly in butter and set aside. Parboil the tarragon and pound it to a paste with butter. In a large skillet, melt this flavored butter and add the onions. Cook until the onions are delicately colored, stirring constantly. Stir in the sour cream and cook for 5 minutes. Stir in the **Coca-Cola®**, and rich chicken broth. Bring this to a boil and simmer for 5 minutes. Place the chicken breasts in the sauce and simmer gently. Season to taste with salt, black pepper and a dash of nutmeg. Serve over rice.

Chicken and Shrimp Jambalaya

4 slices bacon, chopped
1-1/2 cups celery, sliced
1 cup rice
1 cup onion, chopped
1 cup green pepper, chopped
16 ounce can tomatoes
1 cup water
1/2 cup **Coca-Cola®**
1/2 cup catsup
1/2 teaspoon garlic salt
1 teaspoon salt
2 cups chicken, cooked and chopped
2 cups shrimp, cooked and cleaned

In a 3-quart Dutch oven, fry the bacon until crisp. Stir in the celery, rice, onion and green pepper and cook for 5 minutes, stirring frequently. Add the tomatoes, water, **Coca-Cola®**, catsup, garlic salt and salt and mix well. Bring to a boil, then cover and simmer 20 minutes, stirring occasionally. Add the chicken and shrimp and heat thoroughly.

Sweet and Hot Chicken

1/2 cup butter
1/4 cup Worcestershire sauce
1 large clove garlic, minced
1/2 cup red currant jelly
1 tablespoon Dijon mustard
1 cup **Minute Maid®** orange juice
1 teaspoon powdered ginger
3 dashes Tabasco sauce
3 to 3-1/2 pound broiler, quartered

In a saucepan, combine the butter, Worcestershire, garlic, jelly, mustard, orange juice, ginger and Tabasco. Heat gently, stirring constantly, until smooth. Let it cool. Pour the sauce over the chicken in a casserole dish and let it marinate for 3 hours. Cover and cook at 350 degrees for 1 hour. Uncover it and increase the temperature to 450 degrees. Continue cooking, basting frequently, until brown. For better flavor, make this dish a day ahead.

Chicken with Sour Cream Gravy

4 to 6 chicken breasts
1/4 cup butter or margarine
salt and pepper to taste
1 cup **Sprite®**
1/2 cup chopped celery
1 tablespoon dried onion flakes
1 cup sour cream

In a skillet, melt the butter and brown the chicken breasts well. In a bowl, combine the remaining ingredients except the sour cream and pour this mixture over the chicken. Cover and cook for 20 to 30 minutes or until the chicken is tender. Remove the chicken from the skillet. Stir in the sour cream and blend until the gravy is smooth. Return the chicken to the skillet and keep it warm until ready to serve.

Skillet Chicken

3 pound fryer
salt and pepper to taste
paprika to taste
1 can (4 ounces) mushrooms
1/4 cup **Coca-Cola®**
1 can (8 ounces) tomato sauce
1/4 teaspoon thyme
2 green peppers, cut in strips
1 medium onion, sliced

Cut the chicken into serving pieces and sprinkle with salt, pepper and paprika. Drain the mushrooms, reserving the liquid. In a skillet, brown the chicken in a small amount of fat and remove it from the pan. Stir in the **Coca-Cola®**, tomato sauce, mushroom liquid and thyme. Stir until well blended. Add the green peppers, onion, chicken and mushrooms.

Cover and simmer for 25 minutes.

Baked Chicken Breast

4 whole chicken breasts, split
4 tablespoons minced parsley
2 cloves garlic, pressed
1-1/2 cups **Coca-Cola®**
4 tablespoons slivered blanched almonds
1 can cream of chicken soup
1 can cream of mushroom soup

Mix the soups together and add the **Coca-Cola®** and garlic. Place the chicken in a casserole dish and pour the soup mixture over it. Sprinkle the parsley and almonds on top. Cover and cook at 350 degrees for 1-1/2 hours.

Chicken with Artichoke Hearts

4 whole chicken breasts
(boneless, with skin left on)

1/4 cup clarified butter
16 small canned artichoke hearts
2 cups sliced mushrooms
1/2 cup chopped shallots
few slivers of fresh garlic
1 cup **Coca-Cola®**
1 tablespoon arrowroot or flour

Cut the chicken breasts into bite-sized pieces. Saute these pieces in clarified butter, skin side down, turning carefully until they are browned on all sides. Set them aside on a heated platter. In the same pan, saute the artichoke hearts until they are browned. Remove them to the same heated platter. In the same pan, saute the sliced mushrooms, chopped shallots and garlic.

When the mushrooms are tender and the shallots transparent, transfer the chicken and artichoke hearts back to the pan. Add the cup of **Coca-Cola®** and simmer until the chicken is tender. Remove everything from the juices and thicken with arrowroot or flour and pour over chicken mixture.

Baked Chicken

1 chicken, cut into serving pieces
1/2 stick butter or margarine
1 carrot, sliced
1 rib celery, cut into chunks
1 medium onion, sliced
1/2 cup **Coca-Cola®**
1 teaspoon tarragon
1/2 teaspoon salt
pepper to taste

Place the celery, carrot and onion evenly in the bottom of a heavy casserole dish with a tight fitting lid. Place the chicken on top of the vegetables. In a small saucepan, heat the **Coca-Cola®** and butter until the butter melts. Add the tarragon, salt and pepper. Pour this mixture over the chicken.

Cover and bake in oven at 300 degrees for 1-1/2 hours or until chicken is done.

Breast of Chicken Piquante

2 chicken breasts, halved and skin removed
1-1/2 cups **Coca-Cola®**
1/2 cup soy sauce
1/2 cup cooking oil
4 tablespoons water
2 teaspoons ground ginger
2 tablespoons brown sugar
1/2 teaspoon ground oregano
1/4 teaspoon garlic salt

Remove the bones from the chicken (or buy boneless). Place the chicken in a baking pan, meaty side up. In a bowl, mix together the **Coca-Cola®**, soy sauce, oil, water, brown sugar, ginger, oregano and garlic salt; pour this mixture over the chicken. Bake, uncovered, in a 375 degree oven for 1 hour. Serve with rice.

Herbed Chicken

4 chicken breasts
salt and pepper to taste
10-3/4 ounce can cream of chicken soup
3/4 cup **Sprite®**
1/2 teaspoon thyme
1 tablespoon melted butter
1 can water chestnuts, sliced thin
1 can mushrooms
2 tablespoons chopped green peppers

In a bowl, mix the soup, **Sprite®**, thyme, and butter into a sauce and set aside. Sprinkle the chicken with salt and pepper. Place the chicken in a casserole dish and pour the sauce over it. Cover and bake at 350 degrees for 1 hour until tender. Before serving add the water chestnuts, mushrooms and green peppers. Cook again only until these last ingredients are heated thoroughly.

Old Fashioned Barbecued Chicken

1 fryer (3 to 4 pound)
1/2 cup diced celery

3/4 cup chopped onion
3/4 cup vegetable shortening
1/2 cup catsup
1 teaspoon salt
1/8 teaspoon red pepper
1 cup **Coca-Cola®**
2 teaspoons lemon juice
1-1/2 tablespoons prepared mustard

Cut chicken into quarters or pieces and place on a greased rack in a greased shallow pan. Brown onion and celery in shortening. Add remaining ingredients and simmer for 15 minutes covered. Pour 1/4 of mixture over chicken and bake in a 350 degree oven for 1-1/2 hours. Baste every 20 to 25 minutes with 1/4 of sauce. Turn chicken over after 45 minutes.

Chicken Cordon Bleu

4 pounds chicken breasts, halved
salt
8 slices Swiss cheese
3 ounces sliced ham
3 tablespoons butter
1/2 pound fresh sliced mushrooms
1 can cream of mushroom soup
10 ounces **Sprite®**
2 packages (6 ounce size) long grain & wild rice
slivered almonds

Skin and bone chicken breasts. Place each piece between sheets of waxed paper and pound with a mallet into 4x6 inch fillets. Sprinkle with salt. Place one slice of cheese and one slice of ham on each fillet; roll up and tie with string near each end. In a large skillet, melt butter over medium heat. Brown the chicken rolls lightly on all sides and place them in an oblong baking dish. Saute the mushrooms in the skillet, adding more butter, if needed. Combine the soup and **Sprite®**, blend well. Spoon the soup mixture over the chicken. Top with the mushrooms. Bake at 350 degrees for 1 hour. Prepare the rice according to package directions. Serve the chicken rolls on a bed of rice. Spoon the mushrooms and sauce on top and garnish with almonds.

Australian Barbecued Chicken

3 lbs chicken pieces
1/3 cup flour
2 teaspoons salt
1/3 cup oil
1/2 cup finely diced onion
1/2 cup finely diced celery
1/2 cup finely diced green pepper
1 cup catsup
1 cup **Coca-Cola®**
2 tablespoons Worcestershire sauce
1 tablespoon salt
1/2 teaspoon hickory smoked salt
1/2 teaspoon basil leaves
1/2 teaspoon chili powder
1/8 teaspoon pepper

Rinse the chicken pieces and pat dry. Mix the flour and 2 teaspoons of salt and coat the chicken. In a skillet, heat the oil and brown the pieces on all sides. Place the pieces in a 3-quart casserole dish and discard the drippings. Combine the remaining ingredients, mixing well. Spoon the sauce over the chicken, covering all the pieces. Cover and bake at 350 degrees for about 1 1/4 hours or until the chicken is fork-tender. If desired, serve the chicken and sauce on hot cooked rice. Can be prepared ahead and refrigerated until ready to bake.

Cheese and Chicken

2 to 3 pounds chicken parts
salt and pepper, to taste
3 tablespoons butter, melted
10-3/4 ounce can condensed cheddar cheese soup
1/2 cup **Sprite®**
1 clove minced garlic

Preheat the oven to 400 degrees and move the rack to the top part of the oven. Season chicken parts and place chicken, skin side down, in a 12-3/4x9 inch pan. Pour the melted butter over the chicken and bake for 20 minutes. Turn chicken over and continue baking for 20 more minutes. Mix together the **Sprite®**, condensed soup and garlic and pour over the top of the chicken and bake for 20 minutes more.

TURKEY

Turkey Roast

4 pounds rolled turkey roast
1 cup **Sprite®**
1/2 teaspoon salt
1/8 teaspoon pepper
1/8 teaspoon sage
1/8 teaspoon thyme
1/4 cup water
2 tablespoons flour

Place the turkey in a roasting pan. In a bowl, mix the **Sprite®**, salt, pepper, sage and thyme and pour over the meat. Bake as directed on the package, basting occasionally. Remove the roast from the pan and keep it warm. Skim the fat from the broth. To make gravy, measure the broth and return 1 cup to the roasting pan. In a covered jar, shake the water and flour and stir slowly into the broth. Heat to boiling, stirring constantly. Boil and stir 1 minute.

Turkey Teriyaki

32 ounce frozen white meat turkey roast
1/2 cup brown sugar
3/4 cup **Coca-Cola®**
1/2 cup soy sauce
2 tablespoons cooking oil
2 teaspoons vinegar
1 teaspoon ground ginger
1 clove garlic, minced

Partially thaw the turkey roast and cut it into 12 slices. Arrange the slices of turkey in a shallow dish. For the marinade, mix the brown sugar, **Coca-Cola®**, soy sauce, oil, vinegar, ginger and garlic and pour over the turkey slices. Cover and chill about 1 hour. Drain, reserving marinade. Grill the turkey slices over medium coals about 25 minutes; turn and baste often with marinade.

Turkey Breast in Lemon Sauce

1-1/2 pound turkey breast, boneless with skin on
salt and pepper, to taste
2 tablespoons melted butter
1 can (6 ounces) **Minute Maid®** lemonade concentrate
2 teaspoons dry mustard
1 teaspoon paprika
1 teaspoon ginger
1 teaspoon salt
1 teaspoon pepper

Sprinkle the turkey with salt and pepper and place it in a roasting pan. Mix the butter and lemonade concentrate and pour it over the turkey breast. Cover loosely with foil and bake at 350 degrees for 1-1/2 hours or until the turkey is cooked through. Remove the turkey from the pan. Pour the juice into a saucepan and heat until boiling. Whisk in the dry mustard, paprika, ginger, salt and pepper and heat until thickened. Glaze the meat with the sauce. Thinly slice the turkey and serve it with sauce. For a garnish, use lemon wedges.

DUCK

Barbecued Duck

Ducks
salt and pepper

olive oil
sauce (see below)

Split ducks and sprinkle with salt and pepper. Place on the grill, bone side down, over low to medium coals. Baste with olive oil and turn frequently. Leave on bone side 2/3 of time. After approximately 45 minutes, begin to baste with sauce. Continue turning and basting until tender. (Approximately 1-1/2 hours total cooking time.)

Sauce for Barbecued Duck:

> 1-1/2 sticks butter or margarine
> 1/2 cup **Coca-Cola®**
> 1/2 cup catsup
> 1 cup vinegar
> juice of 1 lemon
> 1 garlic clove or 1 teaspoon garlic purée
> 2 tablespoons Worcestershire sauce
> 2 teaspoons seasoned salt
> 1 tablespoon chili powder
> 1 teaspoon celery salt
> Tabasco to taste
> salt and pepper to taste
> 1 teaspoon onion purée

Melt the butter and add the **Coca-Cola®**, catsup, vinegar and lemon juice. Add the remaining ingredients and simmer 15 minutes.

Roast Duck

> 1 duck (Long Island or wild)
> 1 cup **Minute Maid®** orange juice
> 1/2 cup **Coca-Cola®**
> 1 teaspoon salt
> 1 whole orange (preferably seedless)

Truss the duck and place breast side down in covered pan. Combine the orange juice, **Coca-Cola®** and salt and pour it over the duck. Bake 35 minutes per pound at 350 degrees, basting every 10 minutes. Garnish with orange slices.

BEEF

Family Pot Roast

About 3 lbs. chuck roast, any cut
2 tablespoons oil
1 can (16 oz) tomatoes
1 cup **Coca-Cola®**
1 pkg (1 1/2 oz) spaghetti sauce mix
1 cup finely chopped onion
3/4 cup finely chopped celery
1 1/2 teaspoons salt
1/2 teaspoon garlic salt

In a Dutch oven, heat the oil and brown the meat, about 10 minutes on each side. Drain off the fat. In a bowl, break up the tomatoes in their juice and add the remaining ingredients, stirring until the spaghetti sauce mix is dissolved. Pour the sauce over the meat. Cover, simmer slowly about 2 1/2 hours or until meat is fork-tender. Thicken the gravy and serve over sliced meat

Beef Stew in Tomato-Cheese Sauce

2 pounds lean stewing beef, cut into bite size pieces
12 small onions
1 cup celery, chopped
2 large potatoes, cut into eighths
6 carrots, cut into 6 inch pieces
1 slice white bread, cubed
16 ounces (2 cans) tomato sauce with cheese
1 cup **Coca-Cola®**
1-1/2 teaspoons salt
1/8 teaspoon pepper
dill seed
parmesan cheese

Combine all ingredients except the parmesan cheese in a casserole dish. Sprinkle the parmesan cheese on top. Cover, and bake at 250 degrees for 4-1/2 to 5 hours. Do not open the oven door.

Coca-Cola® Roast

1 beef roast
(bottom round, chuck or other less tender cut works well)
12 ounces **Coca-Cola®**
1 package dry onion soup mix

Place the unseasoned roast in a baking dish. Sprinkle the onion soup mix over the roast. Pour in the **Coca-Cola®**. Cover and seal tightly with aluminum foil. Place in oven and cook at 300 degrees until tender. Time will vary with size of roast. (A 4 pound roast will take 3-1/2 to 4 hours.)

Saucy Ribs

1/4 cup dark brown sugar, lightly packed
2 teaspoons dry mustard
2 tablespoons seasoned salt
1/2 teaspoon pepper
2 teaspoons prepared horseradish
1 cup **Coca-Cola®**
1 cup water
6 tablespoons lemon juice
6 tablespoons Worcestershire sauce
1/4 cup cider vinegar
1/2 cup instant minced onion
6 drops Tabasco sauce
6 pounds spareribs

In a saucepan, blend the sugar, mustard, salt and pepper. Stir in the remaining ingredients to make a sauce. Bring to a boil, cover and simmer 10 minutes. In a conventional oven, brown the ribs in a roasting pan at 350 degrees.

Pour off the fat and spoon the sauce over the ribs; cover tightly with foil and cook about 1 hour.

Alternate method: Brown the ribs on both sides in a Dutch oven, heavy skillet, or saucepan. Pour off the fat and pour the sauce over the ribs. Bring to a boil. Cover and simmer for 1 to 1-1/2 hours. Baste and turn the ribs often.

Beef Oriental

1 pound boneless round steak (3/4 inch thick)
1/4 teaspoon ground ginger
2 tablespoons butter or margarine
1-1/2 cups **Coca-Cola®**
16 ounce can Chinese vegetables, drained
1 teaspoon brown sugar
1/2 cup carrots, diagonally sliced
1/2 cup celery, diagonally sliced
1/2 cup green onions, diagonally sliced
10-3/4 ounce can beefy mushroom soup
1 tablespoon cornstarch
1 tablespoon soy sauce
1/2 teaspoon salt

Slice the meat into thin strips. In a skillet or wok, melt the butter and cook the carrots, celery and onions with the ginger until just tender; push them to one side. Add the meat and cook until the color just changes (about 3 to 4 minutes). Add the remaining ingredients and cook, stirring constantly, until thickened. Serve over rice.

This may be prepared ahead. It is especially good served with broccoli spears and baked apples.

Deviled Beef Stew

1-1/2 pounds beef stew meat, cut in 1 inch cubes
1/3 cup all purpose flour
2 tablespoons cooking oil
2 cups water
1 tablespoon dry mustard
1-1/2 teaspoons salt
1 clove garlic, minced
1 teaspoon chili powder
1 teaspoon Worcestershire sauce
1/4 teaspoon pepper
1-1/2 cups **Coca-Cola®**
4 medium potatoes, peeled and quartered

6 small onions, quartered
4 carrots, quartered
2 stalks celery, cut in 1 inch pieces
1/4 cup cold water

In a plastic bag toss the beef cubes with flour to coat, reserving the remaining flour. In a large saucepan or Dutch oven, brown the beef, 1/3 at a time, in hot oil. Return all the meat to the pan and remove from the heat. Add the 2 cups of water, mustard, salt, garlic, chili powder, Worcestershire sauce, and pepper. Simmer, covered, 1 to 1-1/2 hours or until meat is almost tender. Add the **Coca-Cola®**, potatoes, onions, carrots, and celery. Simmer, covered, about 30 minutes or until vegetables are tender.

For gravy, remove the meat and vegetables; skim the fat from the liquid, if necessary. Blend 1/4 cup cold water into the reserved flour until smooth. Slowly stir into the hot liquid. Cook and stir until thickened and bubbly. Season to taste with salt and pepper. Return meat and vegetables to gravy mixture. Heat.

Eye of the Round Roast

1/2 cup soy sauce
1/2 cup **Coca-Cola®**
juice of 2 lemons
bacon slice
2 teaspoons instant marinade
2 teaspoons garlic powder
4 to 5 teaspoons parsley flakes
eye of the round roast

Mix together the soy sauce, **Coca-Cola®**, lemon juice, garlic powder, and parsley flakes and set aside. Rinse the roast and pat dry. Put it into a baking bag, pour the mixture on top, and tie the bag. Leave it out (not in the refrigerator) overnight or at least 4 hours. Twenty minutes before baking, add 2 teaspoons instant marinade. Preheat the oven to 400 degrees, remove the roast from the bag and put it into a roasting pan. Place the slice of bacon on top of the roast.

Bake uncovered for 10 minutes at 400 degrees, then reduce to 300 degrees and cook for 1 hour. Turn off oven and leave until completely cooled.

Pirate Steak

3 pound sirloin steak (1-1/2 to 2 inches thick)
12 ounce can **Coca-Cola®**
1/2 cup chili sauce
1/4 cup salad oil
2 tablespoons soy sauce
1/2 teaspoon red pepper sauce
1 tablespoon Dijon type mustard
1/8 teaspoon liquid smoke
1/2 cup chopped onions
2 cloves garlic, crushed
1 teaspoon salt
1/2 teaspoon pepper

In a pan mix together all the ingredients except the salt, pepper, and steak; simmer for 30 minutes. Brush the meat with the sauce. Place the steak on the grill 4 inches from medium coals. Cook 15 minutes on each side, basting frequently with the sauce. After removing the steak from the grill season it with salt and pepper.

Hawaiian Burgers

1 1/2 pounds ground meat
1 1/2 teaspoons salt
1/4 teaspoon pepper
1 can (13 ounce) pineapple tidbits, drained
2 cloves garlic, minced
1/4 cup **Sprite®**
1/4 cup soy sauce
2 tablespoons catsup
1 tablespoon vinegar
1/4 teaspoon pepper
6 slices bacon

Thoroughly mix the meat, salt and 1/4 teaspoon pepper. Shape into 6 patties and press 5 to 6 pineapple tidbits into each. Combine the garlic, **Sprite®**, soy sauce, catsup, vinegar, and pepper. Place patties in glass dish and pour the sauce over the patties. Cover and refrigerate 30 minutes, turning occasionally. Remove the patties from the marinade. Wrap a bacon slice around each patty and secure with a wooden toothpick. Cook the patties on a rack in a broiler pan about 5 inches from the heat with the oven set on broil or 550 degrees for 12 to 15 minutes. These can be cooked on a grill.

Coca-Cola® Burgers

1 egg
1/2 cup **Coca-Cola®**, divided
1/2 cup crushed saltine crackers
1/4 cup finely chopped onion
6 tablespoons creamy French salad dressing, divided
2 tablespoons grated parmesan cheese
1/4 teaspoon salt
1-1/2 pounds ground beef
6 hamburger buns, split

In a mixing bowl combine the egg, 1/4 cup of **Coca-Cola®**, cracker crumbs, onion, 2 tablespoons of the dressing, cheese and salt. Add the meat and mix well. Form into 6 patties, 3/4 inch thick. For the sauce: Mix the remaining **Coca-Cola®** and dressing. Grill the meat over medium coals about 10 minutes or to desired doneness. Turn once; baste occasionally with sauce.

Serve on buns. Use remaining sauce as topping, if desired.

Sloppy Joes

1 pound ground beef
1 medium onion, chopped
1-1/2 tablespoons flour
1 cup **Coca-Cola®**
2/3 cup catsup
2 tablespoons vinegar
1 tablespoon Worcestershire sauce
2 level teaspoons dry mustard

In a skillet brown the meat and onions. Drain the excess fat. Add the remaining ingredients and stir to mix. Cover and simmer for 30 minutes. Serve hot in hamburger buns.

Sensational Veal Stew

2 to 2-1/2 pounds boneless veal, cut into 1 inch cubes
6 tablespoons butter or margarine
1 pound small white whole onions (16)
12 ounces fresh mushrooms, sliced (4-1/2 cups)
1 clove garlic, minced
1 teaspoon salt
1/8 teaspoon freshly ground pepper
1/3 cup all purpose flour
10-1/2 ounce can condensed chicken broth
3/4 cup **Sprite®**
1 carrot, halved
1 leek, sliced
1 stalk celery, halved
2 sprigs parsley
1/4 teaspoon dried thyme, crushed
1 bay leaf
3 tablespoons lemon juice
2 egg yolks
3/4 cup whipping cream
grated nutmeg
lemon wedges

In a Dutch oven or large saucepan, melt the butter, add the veal and simmer over low heat, uncovered, for about 10 minutes (do not brown). Add the onions, mushrooms, garlic, salt, and pepper; cook, uncovered, 10 minutes more.

Sprinkle the flour over the meat and stir until blended. Add the chicken broth, **Sprite®**, carrot, leek and celery. Place the parsley, thyme, and bay leaf in a cheesecloth bag and add to the mixture. Cover and simmer, stirring occasionally, for 30 minutes or until the meat is tender. Remove and discard the cheesecloth bag, carrot, and celery. Stir in the lemon juice. In a bowl beat together the egg yolks and cream. Stir about 1 cup of the hot mixture into the egg yolk mixture and return it all to the hot mixture, stirring constantly.

Heat until it is bubbly and slightly thickened. Transfer to a serving bowl and sprinkle with nutmeg. Serve with lemon wedges.

Barbecued Pot Roast

4 to 5 pounds beef pot roast
2 teaspoons salt
1/4 teaspoon pepper
2 tablespoons butter
1/2 cup **Coca-Cola®**
8 ounces tomato sauce
3 medium onions, sliced
2 cloves garlic, finely chopped
1 tablespoon brown sugar
1/2 teaspoon dry mustard
1/4 cup vinegar
1/4 cup catsup
1/4 cup lemon juice
1 tablespoon Worcestershire sauce

Rub the pot roast with salt and pepper. In a large pot heat the butter and brown the meat on all sides. Add the **Coca-Cola®**, tomato sauce, onions, and garlic. Cover and cook over low heat for 1-1/2 hours. Mix the remaining ingredients together and pour over the pot roast. Cook slowly for another 1-1/2 hours or until the meat is very tender.

This is great when served with buttered noodles, asparagus spears, garlic bread and a tossed salad.

Garlic Beef

4 pounds beef
garlic cloves
1 stick butter or margarine
2 cups **Coca-Cola®**, divided
1/4 cup water
salt and pepper

Cut the meat in 2 inch cubes. Insert 1 clove of garlic into each piece of meat. Brown in the butter in a skillet. Transfer to a casserole dish and add the water and 1 cup of **Coca-Cola®**. Sprinkle with salt and pepper to taste. Bake in 350 degree oven about 45 minutes. Add remaining **Coca-Cola®** and cook another 15 to 20 minutes, or until tender. Serve on a bed of rice. This freezes well.

Green Pepper Steaks

    1 pound top round steak
    1 tablespoon oil
    1 clove garlic, crushed
    2 onions, coarsely chopped, divided
    salt and pepper
    1/2 teaspoon curry powder
    1 cup **Coca-Cola®**
    1 large green pepper
    6 ounces mushroom slices
    tomato slices for garnish

Cut the meat into 1/2 inch strips after trimming the fat from it. In a large skillet heat the oil, add the garlic and brown the meat well. Add half the chopped onion. Add the salt, pepper, curry powder and **Coca-Cola®**. Simmer, covered for 1 hour. Add more liquid if needed. Cut green pepper in thin strips. In a small pan brown the pepper with the remaining onion in a small amount of oil. Add to the steak. Stir in mushrooms. Simmer 20 minutes more. Top with tomato slices.

Veal Pocketbooks

    6 thin veal steaks (about 1-1/2 pounds)
    6 slices boiled ham
    6 slices Swiss cheese
    2 tablespoons flour
    1/4 teaspoon paprika
    2 tablespoons cooking oil
    1 can cream of mushroom soup
    3/4 cup light cream
    1/2 cup **Sprite®**
    3 tablespoons onion, finely chopped
    hot cooked rice

Mix the flour and paprika and set aside. Trim the cheese and ham slices to cover the lower half of the veal steaks. Fold the veal over to enclose the cheese and ham and carefully dip each piece in the flour mixture. In a large skillet, heat the oil and brown the meat slowly until crusty, being very careful to keep the meat and filling intact. Drain off the excess fat in the pan. Combine the soup, cream, **Sprite®** and onions and pour over the meat. Cover and cook over low heat for 30 minutes. Serve with hot rice.

Forgotten Stew

1 pound lean stew meat
2 potatoes, quartered
2 carrots, sliced
2 onions, quartered
1/2 cup celery, chopped
1 tablespoon tapioca
8 ounces tomato sauce
1/2 cup **Coca-Cola®**

Put the stew meat, potatoes, carrots, onions, and celery in a casserole dish. Sprinkle with tapioca. Combine tomato sauce and **Coca-Cola®** and pour over the top. Cover tightly. Put in 250 degree oven and do not peek for 4 hours.

Meatballs and Sauerkraut

1 pound ground chuck
1 pound ground lean pork
1 teaspoon salt
1/2 cup thick applesauce
1/2 cup dry bread crumbs
2 tablespoons chili sauce
1/8 teaspoon ground allspice
1/8 teaspoon freshly ground black pepper
2 tablespoons oil
2 tart green apples, peeled and cut in eighths
1 large onion, finely chopped
2 pounds drained sauerkraut
3/4 cup **Sprite®**

In a bowl combine the beef, pork, salt, applesauce, bread crumbs, chili sauce, allspice and pepper. Mix lightly and form into 3/4 inch balls. In a large skillet heat the oil and brown the meatballs a few at a time. Set them aside on a paper towel to drain. Saute the apple and onion in the drippings remaining in the skillet until tender. Stir in the sauerkraut and **Sprite®** and bring to a boil. Place the meatballs on top of the sauerkraut, cover and simmer for 30 minutes.

Barbecued Meatballs

1 pound ground lean chuck
1 cup bread crumbs
1/4 cup powdered milk
1 cup catsup
3/4 cup **Coca-Cola®**
1/2 cup onion, chopped
1/2 cup green peppers, chopped
1 teaspoon salt
1/2 teaspoon black pepper
1 tablespoon Worcestershire sauce

Mix meat and bread crumbs and make into balls. Place in a baking dish. Make a sauce of all the remaining ingredients. Pour the sauce over the meatballs. Bake uncovered in 325 degree oven for 1 hour.

Chili

2-1/2 pounds ground lean chuck
3 cloves garlic, crushed
2-1/2 tablespoons chili powder
1/2 medium onion, chopped
1/2 teaspoon black pepper
1 teaspoon salt
2-1/2 teaspoons monosodium glutamate (optional)
1 cup **Sprite®**
3 cups tomato juice

Combine the meat, garlic, onion, pepper, salt and monosodium glutamate in a skillet and brown well. Add the **Sprite®**, chili powder and tomato juice and simmer for 45 minutes or until tender.

This freezes well. When heating frozen chili, add a 4 ounce can of tomato juice and a dash of Tabasco. Let simmer 15 minutes.

Oriental Beef

6 breakfast steaks
meat tenderizer
3 tablespoons cooking oil

1 green pepper
1 red pepper
2 ribs celery
2 small onions, sliced thin
1 cup mushrooms
1 cup water chestnuts

Sauce:

1-1/2 cups **Coca-Cola®**
3/4 teaspoon powdered ginger
3 tablespoons soy sauce
1 beef bouillon cube
2 tablespoons cornstarch

Sprinkle the meat with tenderizer. Cut it into 1/2 inch strips (Note: steaks 1/8 inch thick may be partially frozen and easily cut with kitchen shears). In a skillet heat the oil and brown the beef for 3 minutes. Remove the meat to a dish. Cut the vegetables in diagonal strips and cook for a few minutes in the oil. Combine the **Coca-Cola®**, ginger, soy sauce, bouillon, and cornstarch to make a sauce. Return the meat to the skillet and pour the sauce over the vegetables and meat. Reduce the heat and cook slowly, approximately 30 minutes. Water may be added to achieve desired consistency of sauce. Serve over rice or Chinese noodles.

Spanish Steak

1 round steak, 2 inches thick
4 tablespoons flour
salt and pepper
1 onion, sliced
1 green pepper, sliced
1 small jar pimentos
1 small bottle stuffed olives, with brine
2 cans tomato soup
10 ounces **Coca-Cola®**

Mix the flour, salt and pepper. Dredge the steak in the flour mixture. Place the steak in a large baking dish, cover with the sliced onions, green pepper rings, pimentos and olives. Over this mixture pour the soup and **Coca-Cola®**. Cover and bake at 250 degrees for 2 hours.

This dish is really great with rice.

Barbecued Ribs

3 to 4 pounds ribs
3 tablespoons oil
1 tablespoon salt
1/2 teaspoon red pepper
1/2 teaspoon black pepper
2 onions, chopped
2 tablespoons vinegar
2 tablespoons Worcestershire sauce
3/4 cup catsup
3/4 cup **Coca-Cola®**
1 teaspoon paprika
1 teaspoon chili powder

Sprinkle the ribs with salt and pepper. In a large saucepan, heat the oil and brown the ribs. Mix the remaining ingredients to make a sauce. Pour the sauce over the browned ribs and continue cooking over low heat until tender. You can use pork chops instead of ribs.

Chuck Wagon Steak

1-1/2 pounds round steak
1/3 cup flour
1 teaspoon salt
1/4 teaspoon pepper
3 tablespoons oil
2 bouillon cubes
1 cup hot water
12 ounces **Coca-Cola®**
1/2 cup barbecue sauce
1 tablespoon chili powder
1 bell pepper, diced
1/2 cup stuffed olives, sliced

Mix the flour, salt and pepper. Pound this mixture into the meat. In a large skillet, heat the oil and brown the meat. In a bowl, blend the bouillon cubes in the hot water. Add the **Coca-Cola®**, barbecue sauce, chili powder, bell pepper, and olives. Pour this over the meat. Simmer 1-1/2 to 2 hours until meat is tender.

Perfect Brisket

Whole beef brisket
Bottle of chili sauce
1 package dry onion soup mix
1 can **Coca-Cola®**

Score the underside of the brisket against the grain, so you will know how to slice it after cooking.

Combine all the ingredients in a large roasting pan. Cover and cook slowly at 325 degrees until fork tender (approximately 3 hours).

PORK

Ham Basted with Coca-Cola®

1 ham
1 1/2 cups brown sugar
2 teaspoons dry mustard
1/2 cup dry bread crumbs, very fine
12 ounces **Coca-Cola®**
cloves

Cook your ham according to package directions until it reaches an internal temperature of 160 degrees for a "cook before eating ham" or 140 degrees for a "ready to eat ham."

When cool enough to handle, pull off the skin, cover the top of the ham with a mixture of the brown sugar, dry mustard, and bread crumbs. Score the ham, stud with cloves, pour the **Coca-Cola®** around the ham, cover and bake at 400 degrees for approximately 35 minutes, basting from time to time with the liquid.

When it is done, let it set about 30 minutes before carving. If it is to be served cold later, cover with waxed paper and refrigerate. Cold ham slices better than hot.

A 15 lb. ham should serve about 30 people.

Apple Stuffed Pork Roast

4 to 4-1/2 pound pork rib roast
3/4 cup celery, chopped
1/2 cup onion, chopped
6 tablespoons butter or margarine
3 cups herb-seasoned stuffing mix
1-1/2 cups apple, pared and chopped
3/4 cup **Sprite®**
1/2 teaspoon salt
1/2 teaspoon dried rosemary, crushed

Rib roast should have backbone loosened and 8 pockets cut. In a saucepan, cook the celery and onion in butter until tender, but not brown. In a mixing bowl, toss together the stuffing mix, apple, **Sprite®**, salt, rosemary and celery mixture. Stuff about 1/3 cup into each pocket of the roast. Place the roast, fat side up, in an open roasting pan. Roast in 325 degree oven 2-1/2 hours, until a meat thermometer registers 170 degrees. Bake the remaining stuffing in a small casserole dish for the last 30 minutes of the roasting time. Remove the backbone from the roast and serve.

Barbecued Pork Chops

3 to 4 pounds pork chops
3 tablespoons oil
1 tablespoon salt
1/2 teaspoon pepper
2 onions, chopped
2 tablespoons vinegar
2 tablespoons Worcestershire sauce
3/4 cup catsup
3/4 cup **Coca-Cola®**
1 teaspoon paprika
1/2 teaspoon black pepper
1 teaspoon chili powder

Sprinkle chops with salt and pepper. In a large saucepan heat the oil and brown the chops. Mix the remaining ingredients to make a sauce. Pour sauce over browned chops and cook until tender on top of stove at low heat. You can use ribs instead of pork chops.

Glazed Ham

6 to 7 pound ham (uncooked)
1 cup brown sugar
6 ounce can **Minute Maid®** orange juice concentrate

Place the ham in a baking pan, fat side up. Combine the sugar and juice concentrate and pour about half the mixture over the ham. Cover loosely with foil and bake at 325 degrees for 30 minutes per pound. About 30 minutes before the ham is done, remove it from the oven. Score the fat and spoon the remaining mixture over the ham.

Return it to the oven and bake 30 minutes, uncovered, at 400 degrees.

Cherry-Almond Glazed Pork

3 pound boneless pork loin roast
salt and pepper
10 ounce jar cherry preserves
1/4 cup **cherry Coke®**
2 tablespoons light corn syrup
1/4 teaspoon salt
1/4 teaspoon ground cinnamon
1/4 teaspoon ground nutmeg
1/4 teaspoon ground cloves
1/4 cup toasted slivered almonds

Trim the excess fat from the roast and rub the meat with a little salt and pepper. Place it on the rack in a shallow roasting pan. Insert a meat thermometer and roast, uncovered, at 325 degrees for about 2-1/2 hours.

In a saucepan combine the preserves, **cherry Coke®**, corn syrup, salt, cinnamon, nutmeg, and cloves. Bring to a boil, stirring constantly. Reduce the heat and simmer for 2 minutes. Add the almonds. Keep mixture warm. Spoon some of the mixture over the roast to glaze. Continue cooking about 30 minutes more or until the meat thermometer registers 170 degrees, basting several more times with the glaze mixture. Remove the roast to a carving board. Let it stand 15 minutes before slicing. Serve the remaining glaze as a garnish.

Marinated Pork Loin Roast

1/2 cup soy sauce
1/2 cup **Coca-Cola®**
2 cloves garlic, minced
1 tablespoon dry mustard
1 teaspoon ginger
1 teaspoon thyme, crushed
4 to 5 pound boned, rolled, and tied pork loin roast

In a bowl, combine all the ingredients except the meat. Place the roast in a large clear plastic bag and set it in a deep bowl to steady the roast. Pour in the marinade and close the bag tightly. Let it stand 2 to 3 hours at room temperature or overnight in refrigerator. Occasionally press the bag against the meat in several places to distribute the marinade evenly. Remove the meat from the marinade and place the roast on the rack in a shallow roasting pan. Roast, uncovered, at 325 degrees for 2-1/2 to 3 hours until a meat thermometer registers 175 degrees. Baste occasionally with the marinade during the last hour of roasting time.

WILD GAME

Saucy Venison

1 venison roast
1 package dry onion soup mix
1 bottle chili sauce
12 ounces **Coke®**

Mix dry onion soup mix, chili sauce and **Coke®**. Pour over venison in roasting pan. Cover and bake at 325 degrees for approximately 3 hours. Shred venison with fork or slice thinly.

Serve over rice or noodles.

CHAPTER 3

EGGS

Eggs were always very important in the South. Eggs from chickens supplied many an old time farm family with a nutritious breakfast to begin the long day of never-ending chores. Selling eggs down at the general store brought in a little hard currency that could be used to supplement the farm diet with tasty treats. From the late 19th century on, **Coca-Cola®** was often bought with egg money and, occasionally, even *put in* eggs.

Company Eggs

1/4 cup butter
12 eggs
1/2 cup milk
salt and pepper
1 can mushroom soup
1/4 cup **Coca-Cola®**
1/2 cup cheese, grated

In a bowl, beat together the eggs, milk, salt and pepper. In a frying pan, melt the butter and scramble the eggs. Put the cooked eggs into a buttered casserole dish. Mix the soup, **Coke®** and cheese together and pour over the eggs. Refrigerate at least 6 hours, overnight is better. Bake at 300 degrees for 40 minutes or until hot.

Brunch Party Eggs

3 dozen eggs
2 cans cream of mushroom soup
2 cups mushrooms, sliced
2 cups sharp cheese, grated
1/4 cup **Sprite®**
1/2 cup onion, finely chopped
1/2 cup green pepper, finely chopped
salt and pepper to taste

Using two large skillets, scramble the eggs until just set. Transfer the eggs to a 3-quart casserole dish. Add all the remaining ingredients and mix well. Bake in 350 degree oven for 30 minutes.
Note: May be prepared the day before and refrigerated, covered with foil. Bring to room temperature before baking.

Creamy Eggs

3 tablespoons butter or margarine
3 tablespoons flour
1/4 tablespoon salt
1/8 teaspoon pepper
2 1/4 cups **Coca-Cola®**
3/4 cup powdered milk
6 eggs

In a saucepan, melt the butter over low heat. Blend in flour and seasonings. Cook, stirring constantly, until mixture is smooth and bubbly. Remove from the heat. Add the **Coke®** and milk. Return to heat and cook to boiling. Let it boil for one minute, stirring constantly. Gently stir in eggs until cooked. Serve over hot toast, biscuits or rice.

Eggs Atlanta

6 hardboiled eggs, sliced
8 slices bacon
1/2 cup mayonnaise
1/2 cup **Sprite®**
3 teaspoons powdered milk
1 can cream of mushroom soup
1 teaspoon chopped chives

Fry bacon until crisp. Drain on a paper towel and crumble into small pieces. Mix the **Sprite®** and powdered milk. Blend soup and mayonnaise, adding the **Sprite®** mixture gradually. Stir until well mixed. Add chives, stirring well. Make layers of the resulting mixture and egg slices in a 1-quart baking dish. Sprinkle bacon around edge of dish. Bake at 350 degrees for 20 minutes. Makes 4 servings.

Bacon Omelet with Sprite®

4 eggs, beaten
8 slices bacon
1/4 cup **Sprite®**
1/4 teaspoon salt
1/4 cup chopped green onions
2 tablespoons margarine
1/2 cup grated cheese

While preheating oven to 350 degrees, fry bacon until crisp in a skillet. Place on towel to drain, then crumble into small pieces. Mix the eggs, **Sprite®**, salt and onions in a bowl. Melt margarine in the skillet and cover the bottom with grated cheese. Heat for 30 seconds (or long enough for cheese to start melting). Pour in the egg mixture. Heat until mixture stiffens. Place in the 350-degree oven and cook until top is dry (about 5 minutes). Remove from oven and sprinkle bacon over the top. Cut across the center lightly with a knife and fold. Slide onto a serving platter and garnish as desired.

Oven Baked Eggs

6 eggs
1/2 pound grated sharp cheese
1/4 cup flour
1/2 teaspoon salt
1/4 cup margarine
1/2 cup **Sprite®**
1 1/2 cups milk

In a saucepan, melt margarine, then stir in flour and salt until blended. Slowly add **Sprite®** and milk, stirring until mixture is smooth. Add cheese and stir until it is melted into the mixture. Pour mixture into a 1 1/2-quart casserole dish. Break eggs into the sauce. Bake at 350 degrees until eggs become firm. Serves 6.

Eggs with Celery Sauce

12 hardboiled eggs, quartered lengthwise
1/2 cup chopped celery
1/4 cup chopped pimento
1/3 cup saltine cracker crumbs
2 ounces crumbled blue cheese
1/2 cup **Sprite®**
2 1/2 cups milk
1 teaspoon salt
6 tablespoons flour
7 tablespoons margarine

Start by melting 6 tablespoons of margarine in a saucepan. Blend in flour and salt. Pour in **Sprite®** and milk. Cook, stirring constantly, until thick. Add cheese, pimento and celery. Put the eggs in a 12 x 7-inch baking dish. Put sauce on top. Melt the remaining tablespoon of margarine and mix with the cracker crumbs. Sprinkle around edge of dish.

Bake at 325 degrees for 45 minutes. Serves 4.

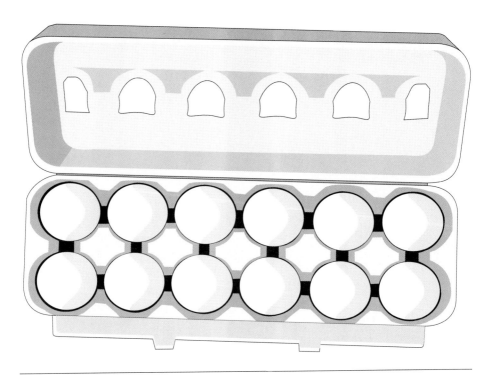

CHAPTER 4

SEAFOOD

Ocean delicacies baked golden brown, shrimp in a spicy sauce . . . all this and more is the bounty of the sea. "With Coca-Cola®" and "in Coca-Cola®"—that's the secret of classic cooking with Coca-Cola®. So cast your net and try these seafood recipes.

Crabmeat Supreme

1 can tomato soup
1/2 cup **Coca-Cola®**
1 cup grated cheddar cheese
1 tablespoon cornstarch
2 tablespoons water
2 cups canned crab meat
1 cup buttered bread crumbs
grated cheese

In a double boiler over hot, not boiling, water heat the soup and **Coca-Cola®**. Add the cheese and cook, stirring constantly, until the cheese melts. Blend the cornstarch and water and add to the soup, cooking until thickened. Add the crab meat. Mix and place in a casserole dish. Top with the buttered bread crumbs and grated cheese to cover. Broil until lightly browned. Serve over wild rice.

Barbecued Oysters

1 pint oysters
flour
3 tablespoons butter (no substitutes)
1/4 cup butter (no substitutes)
1/2 cup **Coca-Cola®**
1/2 cup A-1 steak sauce

Wash the oysters and drain on paper towels. Dip the oysters in flour. In a skillet, melt the 3 tablespoons of butter and brown the oysters. Remove the oysters from the skillet and add the remaining butter, **Coca-Cola®** and A-1 sauce. Stir together. Add the oysters and simmer until oysters are tender.

Seafood Fettucini

3 tablespoons butter
1 small onion, chopped
1/2 pound sea scallops
1/2 pound shrimp, peeled and deveined
1/2 pound mushrooms, chopped
1/2 cup **Coca-Cola®**
1/2 cup water
1 tablespoon lemon juice
3 tablespoons all-purpose flour
1 teaspoon salt
1 cup half-and-half
2 tablespoons grated parmesan cheese
2 tablespoons parsley, chopped
spinach fettucini nests

In a 10-inch skillet, melt the butter over medium heat and cook the onion until tender. Add the seafood, mushrooms, **Coca-Cola®**, water and lemon juice. Reduce heat to medium-low; cover and cook until the seafood is tender, stirring frequently. In a small bowl, blend the flour, salt and half-and-half. Gradually stir in the seafood mixture, stirring constantly until thickened. Fix fettucini according to the package directions. To serve, spoon seafood mixture into the center of the fettucini nests. Sprinkle with parmesan cheese and parsley.

Seafood au Gratin

1/2 pound cooked shrimp
1/2 pound cooked crab meat
1/2 pound cooked lobster
1/2 pound cooked sole
2 tablespoons butter
2 tablespoons flour
3/4 cup milk
1/2 cup grated cheese (parmesan or cheddar)
1/2 cup **Coca-Cola®**
bread crumbs

Cut the seafood into bite-size pieces and arrange the pieces in a baking dish. Mix the butter and flour over low heat and stir in the milk and grated cheese. When slightly thickened, add the **Coca-Cola®**. Pour the sauce over the seafood and top with the bread crumbs. Bake for 20 to 25 minutes at 325 degrees, until browned.

Opal Shrimp Creole

1/2 cup green pepper, chopped
1 cup onion, chopped
1/2 cup celery, chopped
1 clove garlic, minced
3 tablespoons salad oil
2-1/2 tablespoons flour
1 teaspoon salt
1 tablespoon chili powder
1 cup **Sprite®**
2 cups tomato sauce
1 tablespoon vinegar
2 cups cooked shrimp
cooked rice

Saute the pepper, onion, celery and garlic in hot oil until tender. In a bowl, combine the flour, salt, and chili powder. Add the **Sprite®** slowly and mix. Add to the sauteed mixture and mix well. Add the tomato sauce. Simmer uncovered until thick. Add the vinegar and shrimp. Heat thoroughly and serve over hot cooked rice.

Shrimp Jewel Canapeś

2 envelopes unflavored gelatin
1 1/2 cups consomme
1 cup **Coca-Cola®**
dash Tabasco
1/2 teaspoon salt
1/4 teaspoon Worcestershire
30 small shrimp, cooked
30 Melba toast rounds
mayonnaise

Soften the gelatin in 1/2 cup cold consomme. Heat the remaining consomme and add to the gelatin, stirring until dissolved. Cool and add **Coca-Cola®**. Add Tabasco, salt and Worcestershire. Oil 30 small muffin cups (1-1/4 inch bottom diameter); place 1 shrimp in the bottom of each cup. Add just enough gelatin mixture to barely cover shrimp. Chill until firm. Unmold. Spread toast rounds with mayonnaise and top with shrimp aspic. A tiny dab of mayonnaise on top is optional.

South Carolina Shrimp Creole

1 pound fat back, sliced
5 pounds onions
3 or 4 bell peppers
5 pounds shrimp
1 bunch celery
1 can (No. 2) tomatoes
2 cans (10 3/4 ounce) tomato soup
20 ounces **Coca-Cola®**
1 1/2 small bottles catsup
salt to taste
pepper
Worcestershire sauce to taste

In an electric frying pan, fry the fat back and remove it from the pan. Chop the onions, bell peppers, and celery and saute in the grease. Add all of the remaining ingredients except the shrimp. Simmer for 1 1/2 hours, covered. Clean and boil the shrimp. Fifteen minutes before serving, add the shrimp to the mixture and continue simmering. Serve over hot rice. You can make the sauce ahead of time and freeze. Just heat and add the shrimp.

Coca-Cola® Bayou Gumbo

1/2 pound fish fillets
1 cup chicken broth
1/2 cup **Coca-Cola®**
1 cup clam broth
1 (7-ounce) can crabmeat
2 tomatoes, chopped
3 cups cooked rice
1/4 cup onion, chopped
salt and pepper (to taste)
2/3 cup diced carrots
2/3 cup sliced okra

Cut fish into 1-inch pieces and place in a large pot. Add all ingredients except salt, pepper and rice. Bring to a boil. Cover and simmer for 10 to 20 minutes. Add salt and pepper to taste. Place in bowls for serving and top with heaps of rice. Serves 6 to 8.

Scallops and Sprite®

1 1/2 pounds scallops, chopped
1/2 cup **Sprite®**
1/2 teaspoon salt
dash cayenne pepper
1 teaspoon minced onion
3 tablespoons flour
3 tablespoons margarine
1/2 cup heavy cream
1/2 cup buttered crumbs
1 cup grated Cheddar cheese

Mix scallops with **Sprite®**, salt, cayenne pepper and onion in a saucepan. Bring to a boil. Cover and let simmer for 10 minutes. Drain, but keep 1 cup of the liquid. Melt the margarine and blend in flour. Add the cup of liquid and cream. Cook, stirring, until thickened. Add cheese and scallops. Place in 6 individual portion baking dishes and sprinkle on crumbs. Bake at 400 degrees for 10 minutes.

Serves 6.

Coca-Cola® Flounder

1 pound flounder fillets
1/2 cup **Coca-Cola®**
1/3 cup minced onion
1 (4-ounce) can chopped mushrooms
salt and pepper to taste
paprika to taste
1/2 teaspoon curry powder

Place flounder in a buttered baking dish. Sprinkle with onion. Add **Coca-Cola®**, mushrooms (with liquid) and seasonings. Leave uncovered and bake at 350 degrees approximately 30 minutes. Flounder should flake easily when tested with a fork.

Baked Sole in Sprite®

2 pounds sole fillets, skinless, cut to serving size
1/2 cup **Sprite®**
3 cups sliced potatoes
1 teaspoon paprika
1/2 teaspoon salt
1 (4-ounce) can sliced mushrooms, drained
1/4 teaspoon pepper
1 tablespoon grated onion
2 tablespoons flour
1 cup sour cream

Put potatoes in a greased 12 x 8 x 2-inch baking dish and top with mushrooms. Combine the paprika, salt and pepper and sprinkle half the seasoning on the potatoes. Combine the remaining ingredients, except the fish and spread half the mixture over the mushrooms. Place fillets on top of that. Spread remaining seasonings over fillets and pour cream mixture over fish, spreading evenly. Bake at 350 degrees for 35 to 45 minutes. Let cool for 10 minutes after removing from oven. Garnish by sprinkling with parsley, if you like.

Crab Meat Candler

1 pound crab meat
1/2 cup **Coca-Cola®**
4 pimentos, cut into 1-inch pieces
salt and pepper as desired

1 1/2 sticks margarine
1 green pepper, cut into 1-inch pieces
1 large onion, chopped

Saute onion and pepper in margarine. Stir in **Coke®**, crab meat, pimentos and other seasonings. Cover and let steam until pepper and onion are tender. Serve with rice, if you like. Makes 4-6 servings.

Coca-Cola® Fish Stew

1/2 pound salt pork, diced
3 pounds boned fish, flaked
10 ounces **Coca-Cola®**
2 pounds onions, diced
1 (14-ounce) bottle catsup
Worcestershire sauce to taste
4 hardboiled eggs, chopped
1 tablespoon vinegar
salt and pepper to taste
1 teaspoon cayenne pepper
2 cans of tomato soup

Brown salt pork in a skillet and remove, leaving drippings in skillet. Saute onions in drippings until tender. Place remaining ingredients exept the fish and eggs in a kettle. Add the onions. Simmer for 30 minutes. Add fish and simmer for another 30 minutes. Add eggs and serve.

Really Quick Oyster Stew

1 8-ounce can oysters
1 cup **Sprite®**
2 cups milk
3 tablespoons margarine
1/4 teaspoon salt
1 teaspoon chili powder

Place oysters and **Sprite®** in a blender and chop for 2 seconds. Pour into a saucepan and simmer for 2 to 3 minutes, while stirring. Add milk, margarine, and salt, and heat. Do not boil. Stir in chili powder just before serving. Makes 4 servings.

Georgia Sea and Mountain Trout

6 pounds trout fillets
1 pound boiled shrimp, chopped
12 oysters, chopped
1 /2 cup **Sprite®**
6 tablespoons melted butter
3 tablespoons flour
1 bunch green onions, chopped
toast
1/4 cup chopped parsley
cayenne pepper, to taste
salt, to taste

Mix flour and butter in skillet into a smooth paste. Stir in shrimp and add onions, cooking until wilted. Add oysters and simmer for five minutes. Stir in **Sprite®** and remove from heat. Sprinkle trout lightly with salt and pepper to taste. Broil trout until brown on both sides. Place trout on toast and cover with the shrimp mixture. Sprinkle with parsley. Makes 12 servings.

CHAPTER 5
MAIN DISHES

Main dishes include casseroles and other mixtures of meat and vegetables. They are easy to prepare and cook, and make filling meals. Adding **Coca-Cola®** and/or sister products adds flavor and excitment to old favorites, pushing them up the yummy scale toward the truly delicious end!

Hamburger Stroganoff

3 or 4 potatoes, sliced
1 pound ground beef
carrots
1 can English peas, drained
2 onions, sliced
1 can tomato soup
10 ounces **Coca-Cola®**
salt

Place a layer of potatoes on the bottom of a casserole dish. Add a layer of carrots, a layer of peas and a layer of onion. Brown the ground beef and place it on top of the onions. Combine the soup and **Coca-Cola®** and pour over the top. Sprinkle with salt. Cook on stove 1 1/2 hours, stirring occasionally. (This is an ideal recipe for a crock pot.)

Lasagna

4 tablespoons vegetable oil
1 1/2 cups onion, chopped
1 tablespoon garlic, chopped
1 1/2 pounds ground chuck
1 teaspoon oregano leaves
1 teaspoon basil leaves
1 bay leaf
2 teaspoons salt, divided
1 1/4 teaspoons pepper, divided
2 cans (28 ounce size) tomatoes
15 ounce can tomato juice
6 ounce can tomato paste
1 cup **Sprite®**
1 pound ricotta cheese
2 eggs
1/2 cup parsley
12 ounces mozzarella cheese
8 tablespoons parmesan cheese
1 pound lasagna noodles

In a saucepan, heat the oil, add the onion and garlic. Saute over medium heat for 5 minutes. Add the meat and cook until brown, breaking up large clumps of meat. Stir in the oregano, basil, bay leaf, half the salt and pepper. Add the tomatoes, tomato sauce, tomato paste and **Sprite®**. (Break up tomatoes in blender.) Heat to boiling, reduce heat and simmer uncovered 60 minutes, stirring occasionally.

Meanwhile, to make the ricotta filling: In a large bowl, combine the ricotta, eggs, and remaining salt and pepper. Beat with a spoon until smooth. Stir in the parsley, 8 ounces of mozzarella, diced, and 4 tablespoons parmesan and set aside.

Cook the lasagna noodles and drain. Preheat the oven to 350 degrees. Lightly grease two 7x11x2 inch baking dishes. Remove the bay leaf from the meat sauce. Spoon a little meat sauce in the bottom of each. Layer the noodles, cheese mixture and meat sauce in the pans, ending with sauce. Sprinkle with the remaining Parmesan cheese and top with the remaining mozzarella cheese, sliced. Bake 45 to 60 minutes. Remove from oven and let set 5 minutes.

You may prepare ahead and refrigerate before baking. When you do, add 15 minutes to baking time.

Shipwreck Casserole

> 1 1/2 tablespoons cooking oil
> 1 large onion, sliced
> 1 pound ground beef
> 1/4 cup rice (uncooked)
> 2 to 3 celery stalks, chopped
> 1 green pepper, chopped
> 1 layer sliced potatoes
> salt and pepper to taste
> 1 can red kidney beans, drained
> 1 can tomato soup (do not dilute)
> 10 ounces **Coca-Cola®**

Spread the cooking oil in the bottom of a 9x13 inch baking dish. Layer the ingredients in the order listed, pouring the can of **Coca-Cola®** evenly over the top. Cover with foil and bake at 350 degrees for 1 hour.

Chili Casserole

> 4 ounces lasagna noodles
> 2 cans (15 ounce size) chili con carne (without beans)
> 1/2 cup **Coca-Cola®**
> 1/2 cup chili sauce
> 1/8 teaspoon pepper
> 8 ounces mozzarella cheese, sliced
> 1 cup cream style cottage cheese
> 1/3 cup grated parmesan cheese

Cook the lasagna noodles according to package instructions. Drain and set aside. In a saucepan, combine the chili, **Coca-Cola®**, chili sauce and pepper and heat through. Layer 1/3 of noodles into a shallow baking pan. Add layer of 1/3 chili mixture and 1/3 each kind of cheese. Repeat layers twice.

Bake covered at 350 degrees for 25 minutes, then 5 minutes uncovered.

Chicken With Wild Rice

1 whole fryer chicken (2-3 pounds.)
1 cup water
1 cup **Coca-Cola®**
1 1/2 teaspoons salt
1/2 teaspoon curry powder
1 medium onion, sliced
1/2 cup celery, sliced
1 pound fresh mushrooms
1/4 cup butter or margarine
2 (6 ounce) packages long grain and wild rice with seasoning
1 cup sour cream
1 can cream of mushroom soup

Place the chicken in a deep kettle and add the water, **Coca-Cola®**, salt, curry powder, onion, and celery. Cover and bring to a boil. Reduce heat and simmer for 1 hour. Remove from heat and strain the broth. Refrigerate the chicken and broth at once, without cooling first. When the chicken is cool, remove the meat from the bones and cut into bite-size pieces. Rinse the mushrooms and pat dry. Slice and saute in butter until golden, about 5 minutes, stirring constantly. Save the liquid with the mushrooms. Measure the chicken broth and use as part of the liquid for cooking the rice, following directions on the package. Combine the chicken, mushrooms and rice in a 3 1/2 to 4 quart casserole dish. Blend the sour cream and soup and toss with the chicken and rice mix. Cover and refrigerate overnight if desired. To heat, bake, covered, at 350 degrees for 1 hour. The casserole may be frozen ahead of time.

Easy Paella

1/2 pound sweet or hot Italian sausage
(if you use links, remove casing)
2 tablespoons olive oil
6 large chicken drumsticks or thighs
14 ounce can stewed tomatoes
2/3 to 3/4 cup regular rice (uncooked)
1 medium green pepper, cut into strips
1 onion, sliced
1 clove garlic, finely chopped

1/2 teaspoon red pepper
> (not necessary if you use hot sausage)

salt

pepper

1/2 cup frozen tiny peas

1 cup **Sprite®**

In a 12-inch skillet over medium high heat, brown the sausage and chicken in oil, stirring to break up the sausage. Add the stewed tomatoes (with their liquid), uncooked rice, green pepper, onion, garlic, salt, peppers, and **Sprite®**. Turn the heat up to high and heat to boiling. Reduce the heat to low, cover and simmer, stirring occasionally, until the chicken and rice are tender and the liquid is absorbed (about 20 minutes). Gently stir in the frozen peas. Heat through.

Baked Ham and Sweet Potatoes

1 smoked ham slice (about 1 pound), cut about 1 inch thick

whole cloves

2 tablespoons brown sugar

2 tablespoons fine dry bread crumbs

1 teaspoon grated orange peel

1/2 teaspoon dry mustard

1 orange

3/4 cup **Minute Maid®** orange juice

maraschino cherries, halved

parsley sprigs

sliced cooked sweet potatoes

Place the ham slice in an 11x7x2 inch baking dish. Insert the cloves in the ham slice at 1 inch intervals. In a bowl, mix the brown sugar, bread crumbs, orange peel, and dry mustard. Sprinkle over the ham. Rinse the orange and cut into 1/4 inch slices. Arrange the slices on top of the ham over the sugar mixture. Carefully pour the orange juice over the top of the ham slice.

Bake at 300 degrees about 40 minutes.

Garnish the ham with maraschino cherries, parsley, and sliced cooked sweet potatoes.

Orange Chops with Rice Tango

4 to 6 pork chops (about 1 inch thick)
3 envelopes instant chicken broth
1/4 teaspoon black pepper
1/4 teaspoon ginger
1 medium onion, thinly sliced
2 cups **Coca-Cola®**
1 cup **Minute Maid®** orange juice
1/4 cup catsup
2 tablespoons brown sugar
2 teaspoons dry mustard
1/2 teaspoon salt
1 cup uncooked rice

Season the pork chops with 1 envelope of chicken broth, pepper, and ginger. In a large skillet, brown the chops on both sides. Remove the chops and drain the excess fat. Add the onion to the skillet and saute lightly. Stir in the **Coca-Cola®**, orange juice, catsup, brown sugar, dry mustard, salt, and remaining chicken broth. Bring to a boil. Stir in the rice and place the chops on top. Cover, lower the heat and simmer for 30 minutes.

Chicken Casserole

1 can cream of celery soup
1/2 cup mayonnaise
2 cups **Sprite®**
2 cups chicken, cooked and diced
1 package white and wild rice
1 pound can French style green beans, not drained
1 medium onion, chopped
1 medium jar pimento, chopped
1 can water chestnuts, sliced
salt and pepper to taste

In a large mixing bowl, combine the soup, mayonnaise, and **Sprite®** and mix well. Stir in the chicken, rice, green beans, onion, pimento, water chestnuts, and salt and pepper. Place in a greased casserole dish and bake at 350 degrees for 1 hour.

Clam and Spaghetti Casserole

2 tablespoons flour
dash of pepper
4 tablespoons margarine
1 can mushroom soup
1/4 cup **Sprite®**
2 cans (7 ounce size) minced clams
1 package (8 ounces) spaghetti
1/2 cup dry bread crumbs

In a saucepan, melt 2 tablespoons of margarine and blend in flour and pepper. Add the soup, **Sprite®**, and clams. Cook, stirring constantly, until thick. Cook spaghetti according to the package directions and drain. Combine with the clam sauce, then put the mixture into a well greased 1 1/2 quart casserole dish. Melt remaining margarine and combine it with bread crumbs, then sprinkle lightly over casserole. Bake at 400 degrees for 10 minutes or until crumbs are lightly browned.

Elegant Seafood Casserole

2 slices bread, cubed
2 cans crab meat
2 cans shrimp, drained
1/2 cup onion, chopped
1/2 cup celery, chopped
1 tablespoon parsley, chopped
1 teaspoon salt
1/2 teaspoon curry powder
1 tablespoon dry mustard
1 teaspoon Worcestershire sauce
1 teaspoon capers, minced
1/2 cup **Coca-Cola®**
1 cup mayonnaise
1/2 cup water

Grease the casserole dish and spread the bread cubes in the bottom. Cover with the crab and shrimp. In a skillet, saute the onion, celery and parsley in a small amount of fat or oil until soft. In a bowl, combine the sauteed vegetables with the remaining ingredients and mix well. Pour the vegetables over the crab and shrimp. Bake at 325 degrees for 30 minutes. Serve hot.

Lobster Casserole

2 packages (9 ounce size) frozen artichokes
seasoned salt to taste
2 packages (4-1/2 ounce size) precooked rice
3 cans (5 ounce size) lobster
2 cans cream of mushroom soup
10 ounces water
10 ounces **Coca-Cola®**
sliced cheese
chopped parsley or chives

Cook the artichokes according the package directions and drain.
Place in a 3 quart casserole dish and sprinkle with seasoned salt.
Cover with a layer of rice.

Drain the lobster and place it over the rice. Blend the mushroom soup
with the water and **Coca-Cola®** and pour it over the lobster.

Bake at 400 degrees for 40 minutes or until the sauce is bubbly. Cut
slices of cheese in half to form triangles and arrange these over the
casserole. Sprinkle with parsley.

Lobster Noodle Casserole

10 rock lobster tails
1/2 cup butter
1/4 cup flour
2 1/2 teaspoons salt
1 1/2 teaspoons paprika
1/2 teaspoon pepper
1 teaspoon instant minced onion
1 teaspoon angostura bitters
4 cups milk
1 cup cream
1/2 cup **Coca-Cola®**
1 package (12 ounce) broad noodles
buttered bread crumbs
1/4 cup capers, drained

Cook the lobster according to the package directions. Slice each tail in half lengthwise and remove the meat from the shell. Cut half of the lobsters into chunks. Set aside.

In a saucepan, melt 1/4 cup butter and stir in the flour, salt, paprika, pepper, onion and bitters. Add the milk and cream and cook until thickened, stirring constantly. Add the **Coca-Cola®** and the lobster chunks.

Cook the noodles according to the package directions. Stir in the lobster mixture. Place in a 3 quart casserole dish and cover with buttered bread crumbs.

Bake at 375 degrees for about 30 minutes or until bubbly. Top with the lobster halves in a pinwheel design.

Melt the remaining butter and stir in the capers. Pour over the lobster halves and bake for 10 minutes longer.

Asparagus and Shrimp

2 medium cans asparagus
1 1/2 cups cooked rice
1 can sliced mushrooms, drained
1 1/2 pounds shrimp, cleaned and cooked
1 can pimento strips, drained
1 can cream of mushroom soup
pepper to taste
1/2 cup **Sprite®**
3 tablespoons powdered milk
1 cup grated cheddar cheese

Drain the asparagus and reserve 1/4 cup liquid. Place the rice in a greased shallow casserole dish and place the asparagus on the rice.

Spread the mushrooms over the asparagus, then add the shrimp and pimentos.

In a bowl, combine the soup with the pepper, powdered milk, **Sprite®**, and reserved liquid and pour over the layers in the casserole dish. Sprinkle with cheese.

Bake at 400 degrees for about 20 minutes or until brown.

Halibut with Vegetables

4 carrots, sliced thin
4 slices bacon
1 large onion, chopped
1/4 pound mushrooms, chopped
2 tablespoons parsley, chopped
3 tablespoons celery, minced
1 teaspoon dill, chopped
2 teaspoons salt
pepper
2 pounds halibut fillets
4 slices lemon
1/4 cup butter
1 cup **Coca-Cola®**

Place the bacon in the bottom of a shallow casserole dish and cover with the carrots. Spread the onion and mushroom over the carrots. Sprinkle with the parsley, celery, dill, 1 teaspoon salt and pepper. Place the halibut on top and sprinkle with the remaining salt. Place the lemon slices over halibut, then dot with butter and pour **Coca-Cola®** over all.

Cover tightly with foil and bake at 400 degrees for 20 minutes. Remove the foil and bake for 20 additional minutes.

CHAPTER 6
VEGETABLES

Vegetables are nutritious and delicious foods, even carrots—although some would disagree. In fact, we had to make our coauthor put carrots back into one recipe. He says you can remove the carrots, if you like. We hope you will try these tasty veggie recipes, even if you are not a vegetable-lover. They really are good!

Easy Baked Beans

1 28 oz. can of pork and beans
1 onion, chopped fine
1 green pepper, chopped fine
1 tomato, chopped fine
1/2 cup dark brown sugar
1/3 cup **Coca-Cola®**
1/8 teaspoon ground cloves

Preheat oven to 250 degrees. Drain the liquid from the pork and beans. Pour into baking dish. Add the onion, pepper and tomato and gently mix. In a bowl, combine the sugar, **Coca-Cola®**, and cloves, stirring until the sugar is dissolved. Pour evenly over the bean mixture. Bake, covered, 30 minutes.

Slow-Cooked Baked Beans

1 can pinto or red beans
6 ounces **Coca-Cola®**
diced onion to taste (approx. 1/2 cup)
diced green pepper (approx. 1/4 cup)
1/4 cup brown sugar
2 tablespoons mustard
1/4 cup catsup
6-8 strips of bacon

In a cast iron skillet, saute 2 strips of bacon with the onion and green pepper until the onion is golden. Stir in all of the other ingredients, except the remaining bacon. Bring to a low boil. Pour into a greased casserole dish. Place the remaining bacon strips across the beans. Bake at 325 degrees for 45 to 50 minutes.

Pot O' Pintos

2 cups dried pinto beans
1 small piece of salt pork
5 dried chili peppers
1 small onion, chopped
5 cups water
6 ounces **Coca-Cola®**
1/2 tablespoon salt

Mix the beans, water, onion, and salt pork in a crock pot or bean pot and cook overnight. Add **Coca-Cola®**, chili peppers, and salt, and cook for several hours more.

Ralph's Favorite Baked Beans

2 cans pork and beans
1 cup brown sugar
1/2 cup catsup
1/2 cup **Coca-Cola®**
1 small onion, diced
2 teaspoons dry mustard
sliced bacon, diced

Mix the beans, brown sugar, catsup, **Coca-Cola®**, onion and mustard and place in a casserole dish. Dot the top with bacon. Bake at 300 degrees, uncovered, for about 1 1/2 to 2 hours.

Sweet Potato Pudding

1/3 cup butter
4 cups grated raw sweet potatoes
1/2 cup powdered milk
1/4 teaspoon salt
1/2 cup honey
1/2 cup chopped nuts
1 cup raisins
1/2 teaspoon cloves
1 teaspoon allspice
1 teaspoon cinnamon
1 1/2 cups **Sprite®**
3 eggs, well beaten

Preheat the oven to 350 degrees. In a medium-sized saucepan, melt the butter and add all of the other ingredients, except the eggs. Place over low heat, and stir until the mixture is well-heated. Add the eggs slowly, stirring constantly. Pour the mixture into a greased 2-quart casserole dish and bake for 30 to 40 minutes. Serve hot or cold, with light cream, if desired.

Sweet Potato Casserole

1/2 cup brown sugar, divided
2/3 cup **Minute Maid®** orange juice, divided
1/3 cup margarine, melted and divided
2 cans (1 pound size) sweet potatoes
2 eggs
1 teaspoon salt
1/4 teaspoon cloves
1 teaspoon ground cinnamon
1 cup chopped pecans

In a bowl, combine 1/4 cup brown sugar, 2 tablespoons butter and 2 teaspoons orange juice and set aside to use for a glaze topping. Whip the potatoes until smooth and beat in the eggs. Add the remaining sugar, orange juice, and butter. Add the salt, cloves and cinnamon. Mix well and pour into a buttered 1 1/2-quart casserole dish. Sprinkle the pecans on top and drizzle the glaze over the pecans. Bake at 350 degrees for 40 minutes.

Sweet Potatoes with Orange Sauce

6 medium sweet potatoes
1 stick margarine
1 cup sugar (white or brown)
2 tablespoons flour
pinch of salt
1 3/4 cups **Minute Maid®** orange juice

Boil or bake the sweet potatoes until almost done. Peel, slice, and place in a baking dish. In a saucepan, combine the margarine, sugar, salt and flour. Cook over low heat until dissolved. Add the orange juice and continue cooking until thickened. Pour over the potatoes. Bake at 350 degrees for 20 minutes.

Sweet Tater Pie

2 cups sweet potatoes, cooked and mashed
1 cup **Sprite®**
1/3 cup powdered milk
1 egg
3/4 cup sugar
1/2 stick margarine, melted
1 teaspoon vanilla
1/2 teaspoon allspice
pinch salt
2 baked pie shells

Mix all the ingredients together and pour into pie shells. Bake at 325 degrees until firm, about 30 minutes.

Candied Sweet Potatoes

4 medium sweet potatoes, peeled
3/4 cup sugar
3 tablespoons flour
2 cups **Sprite®**
butter

Slice the potatoes about 1/4 inch thick. Place in a pan with enough cold water to cover and cook until tender but not done. Drain; transfer the potatoes to a casserole dish. In a bowl, combine the sugar and flour, add the **Sprite®**. Pour the mixture over the potatoes. Dot with butter. Cook at 375 degrees for 30 minutes or until the liquid is thick.

Golden Carrot Bake

3 cups shredded carrots (1 pound)
1 1/2 cups **Coca-Cola®**
2/3 cup long grain wild rice
1/2 teaspoon salt
2 cups shredded American cheese (8 ounces)
1 cup milk
2 beaten eggs
2 tablespoons minced dried onion
1/4 teaspoon pepper

In a saucepan, combine the carrot, **Coca-Cola®**, rice and salt and bring to a boil. Reduce the heat and simmer, covered for 25 minutes. Do not drain. Stir in the milk, eggs, onion, pepper, and 1 1/2 cups of the shredded cheese. Turn the carrot-rice mixture into a 1 1/2 quart casserole dish. Bake uncovered in a 350 degree oven for about 1 hour. Top with the remaining 1/2 cup of shredded cheese.

Return to the oven for about 2 minutes to melt the cheese.

Carrot Crunch

1 medium bunch carrots, sliced
1 teaspoon onion, minced
1 egg
1 cup **Sprite®**
1/3 cup powdered milk
1 tablespoon butter, melted
1/2 cup cracker crumbs
1/4 teaspoon salt
1/4 teaspoon seasoned salt

Cook the carrots and onion together, then mash. Add the egg, milk and **Sprite®** and beat thoroughly. Add the remaining ingredients and put in a buttered casserole dish. Sprinkle with additional butter and cracker crumbs. Bake at 350 degrees for 25 minutes.

Orange Ginger Carrots

        5 medium carrots
        1 teaspoon cornstarch
        1/4 teaspoon ginger
        2 tablespoons margarine
        1 tablespoon sugar
        1/4 teaspoon salt
        1/4 cup **Minute Maid®** orange juice

Slice the carrots about 1 inch thick. Cook, covered, in boiling salted water for about 20 minutes, until barely tender. Drain. In a small saucepan, combine the sugar, cornstarch, salt, and ginger. Add the orange juice, stirring constantly over medium heat until the mixture thickens and bubbles. Boil for 1 minute. Stir in the butter and pour over the hot carrots. Toss to coat evenly.

Steamed Carrot Pudding

        2 medium carrots, cut up
        2 medium apples, peeled, cored and cut up
        1 medium potato, peeled and cut up
        4 ounces suet, cut up
        1 cup sugar
        1/2 cup **Minute Maid®** orange juice
        1 beaten egg
        1 teaspoon vanilla
        1 1/2 cups all purpose flour
        1 1/2 teaspoons baking soda
        1 teaspoon ground cinnamon
        1 teaspoon ground nutmeg
        1/2 teaspoon ground cloves
        1/2 teaspoon salt
        1 cup snipped, pitted dates
        1 cup raisins
        brown sugar sauce (see top of page 89)

Grease a 2 quart mold. Grind together the carrots, apples, potato and suet. Combine the sugar, orange juice, egg and vanilla and stir into the carrot mixture. Stir together the flour, soda, spices, and salt and stir into the carrot mixture. Fold in the dates and raisins. Pour the batter into the mold and cover with foil. In a deep kettle, put enough water to be 1-inch deep. Place the mold on a rack in the kettle. Bring the water to a boil. Cover the kettle and steam for 3-1/2 hours, adding more water, if needed. Remove the mold from the kettle. Cool for 10 minutes and unmold. Serve warm with the Brown Sugar Sauce.

Brown Sugar Sauce:

> 1/2 cup packed brown sugar
> 2 teaspoons cornstarch
> 1/3 cup water
> 2 tablespoons butter
> 1 egg, beaten
> 1 teaspoon vanilla

In a saucepan, mix the brown sugar and cornstarch; stir in the water and butter. Cook and stir until thickened and bubbly. Next, gradually stir 1/2 cup of the hot mixture into the beaten egg and then return it to the saucepan. Cook and stir 1 minute more. Stir in the vanilla.

Green Bean Casserole

> 1 stick butter or margarine
> 3 medium onions
> 4 tablespoons flour
> 1/2 cup powdered milk
> 1 1/2 cups **Sprite®**
> dash Tabasco
> 4 teaspoons soy sauce
> salt to taste
> pepper to taste
> 12 ounces medium cheddar cheese, grated
> 1 can water chestnuts, sliced thinly
> 1 can mushroom stems and pieces
> 3 cans French style green beans

In a heavy skillet, saute the onions in butter. Add the flour, powdered milk, **Sprite®**, Tabasco, soy sauce, salt, pepper, and most of the cheese (save some of the cheese for the top). Drain and add the water chestnuts, mushrooms and green beans. Pour everything into a casserole dish and sprinkle with the remaining cheese. Bake at 350 degrees for 20 to 30 minutes. Freezes well.

Vegetable Goulash

1 medium onion, chopped
1 quart small okra pods
1 medium potato, chopped small
2 cups **Sprite®**
salt and pepper
4 slices salt pork
8 to 10 large tomatoes, peeled and chopped
1 quart young, green butterbeans, cooked
6 ears corn
dash red pepper

Place the onion, okra, potato, **Sprite®**, seasonings, salt pork, tomatoes and cooked butterbeans in a large pot. Cook over low heat 60 to 90 minutes, stirring occasionally. Scrape the corn from the cobs and add it to the goulash. Cook another 15 to 20 minutes.

Brown Rice Pilaf

4 slices of bacon
1/2 cup celery, chopped
1 cup brown rice, uncooked
1/4 cup slivered almonds, toasted
1/2 cup onion, chopped
3 cups beef broth
1/2 cup **Coca-Cola®**
1/2 teaspoon salt

Cook the bacon until crisp; drain, reserving 2 teaspoons of the drippings. Crumble the bacon and set aside. Cook the onions and celery in the reserved drippings until tender but not brown. Stir in the broth, rice, **Coca-Cola®**, almonds, salt and bacon; heat to boiling. Bake, covered, in a 325 degree oven for 1 hour.

Wild Rice au Coca-Cola®

1 cup instant wild rice
1 cup grated cheddar cheese
1 cup ripe olives, chopped
16 ounce can tomatoes

1 cup mushrooms, fresh or canned
salt and pepper to taste
1/2 cup finely chopped onions
1/4 pound butter, melted
1 cup **Coca-Cola®**

Reserve one half of the cheese for topping. In a bowl, combine the other half of the cheese with all the other ingredients. Place the mixture into a 2-1/2 quart casserole dish and top with the remaining cheese. Bake at 350 degrees for 1 hour.

Oven Baked Orange Rice

3/4 cup regular long grain rice
2/3 cup celery, chopped
2 tablespoons onion, chopped
2 tablespoons melted butter
1 tablespoon orange peel, grated
1 teaspoon salt
3/4 cup **Minute Maid®** orange juice
1 1/4 cups water

Preheat the oven to 350 degrees. Mix the rice, celery, onion, butter, orange peel and salt together and pour into a buttered 1-quart casserole dish. In a saucepan, heat the orange juice and water together to boiling. Add the orange juice mixture to the casserole dish and stir. Cover and bake about 45 minutes or until the rice is fluffy and tender. Toss with a fork and sprinkle with chopped parsley or slivered almonds.

Rice and Squash Casserole

2 cups squash
1/4 pound butter
1 cup cooked rice
1/2 onion, finely chopped
1 cup **Sprite®**
1 teaspoon salt
1/2 can cream of mushroom soup
bread crumbs
1/4 cup grated cheddar cheese

Cook, drain and chop the squash. Melt the butter in a casserole dish and add the cooked rice. Add the squash and onions in layers. In a bowl, mix the **Sprite®**, salt and soup and pour it over squash mixture. Top with bread crumbs and cheese. Bake 1 hour at 325 degrees.

Be really refreshed

Pause for Coke! Everybody loves Coca-Cola...for the cold crisp taste that so deeply satisfies.

SERVE *Coca-Cola*

SIGN OF GOOD TASTE

An ad from the Autumn 1959 issue of *Pause for Living*.

CHAPTER 7
SOUPS

There is nothing so wondrously good on a cold winter's day as a hot, steaming bowl of nourishing soup. We offer you several lip-smacking soup recipes in this chapter, all flavor-enhanced with **Coca-Cola®** or sister products of The Coca-Cola Company. The Vegetable Soup Goulash below is just the first of these soups that please your palate and stick to your ribs.

Vegetable Soup Goulash

1 pound ground beef
1 medium onion, chopped
1 package vegetable soup mix
1 pkg (8 oz) skinny egg noodles
1 cup **Coca-Cola®**
1 1/2 cups water
1 can tomatoes (with juice)
bread crumbs

In a large skillet, brown the ground beef and onion. Add the vegetable soup mix, egg noodles, **Coca-Cola®**, water and tomatoes. Simmer, covered, until the liquid is absorbed, stirring occasionally. Transfer to a casserole dish. Top with bread crumbs and bake at 325 degrees for 20 to 30 minutes.

Potato Cheese Soup

3 cups potato cubes
1 cup **Sprite®**
1/2 cup sliced celery
1/2 cup sliced carrots
1/4 cup chopped onion
1 teaspoon parsley flakes
1/2 teaspoon salt
dash pepper
1 chicken bouillon cube
1 1/2 to 2 cups milk
2 tablespoons flour
1/2 pound Velveeta cheese, cubed

Simmer the potato, **Sprite®**, celery, carrots, onion, parsley, salt, pepper, and bouillon cube together for 15 to 20 minutes. Mix the flour and milk together. Gradually add the milk mixture to vegetables, heating until soup thickens and boils. Add cheese and stir until melted.

Vegetable Soup

3 cups chicken broth
2 cups canned tomatoes, drained and roughly chopped
1 onion, chopped
1 garlic clove, chopped
1/2 teaspoon chili powder
1 cup **Coca-Cola®**
2 carrots, peeled and sliced
pinch of cayenne pepper
2 stalks celery, chopped
3 medium zucchini, sliced
2 tablespoons chopped parsley
1 1/2 cups yellow corn
salt to taste
pepper to taste

Combine all of the ingredients and bring to a boil over medium heat. Cook until the vegetables are tender. Garnish with Parmesan cheese and parsley.

Ground Beef Vegetable Soup

1 pound ground beef
1 tablespoon margarine
1 large onion, chopped
4 Irish potatoes, diced
1/3 cup uncooked rice
1 can tomato sauce
2 cups water
1 cup **Coca-Cola®**
1 large can tomato juice
1 small can peas and carrots
1 tablespoon salt
1/2 teaspoon pepper
1 tablespoon Worcestershire
dash Tabasco

In a Dutch oven, brown the ground beef lightly in margarine over low heat, stirring often. Mix in the remaining ingredients and bring to a boil. Reduce heat to simmer and cook for about 2 hours until the desired thickness is achieved. Adjust the seasoning, if necessary.

Fish Chowder

1 1/2 cups onion, diced
1 strip bacon, diced
1/2 cup butter
1 cup **Coca-Cola®**
1 1/2 cups hot water
5 teaspoons salt
1 teaspoon pepper
2 tablespoons Worcestershire
1/4 teaspoon red pepper flakes
1 teaspoon hot sauce
1/4 cup sugar
2 large cans whole tomatoes
5 cups coarsely diced potatoes
1 to 2 boneless skinless mullet fillets (or any oily fish)

Saute the bacon. Add the butter and onions and saute until tender. Add all of the remaining ingredients, except the potatoes, and bring to a boil, then add the potatoes and cook until done, approximately 3 hours. The longer it cooks the better it is. Good with French Bread.

Lentil Super Soup

1 pound dried lentils
2 medium onions, chopped
1 stick celery, diced
1 tablespoon parsley, chopped
16 ounce can stewed tomatoes
2 beef bouillon cubes
6 cups water
2 cups **Coca-Cola®**
1 tablespoon salt
3/4 teaspoon liquid hot pepper sauce
1 pound frankfurters
1 teaspoon oil

Pick over the lentils, wash and drain. Combine all the ingredients, except the frankfurters and oil, in a 5- or 6-quart saucepan. Cover and simmer over low heat for 2 hours, stirring occasionally. In a skillet, heat the oil and brown the frankfurters. Slice the frankfurters and add to the soup and cook 10 minutes longer.

Variation: A ham bone or beef bone may be used in the cooking water. If used, omit the bouillon cubes.

Minestrone

2 tablespoons vegetable oil
2 stalks celery, diced
1 large carrot, diced
1 medium onion, chopped
1 clove garlic, minced
1/2 small head green cabbage, sliced
2 cups **Coca-Cola®**
4 cups water
1 can (16 ounces) whole tomatoes, crushed
2 chicken bouillon cubes
1 1/2 teaspoons salt
1/2 teaspoon dried basil
1/4 teaspoon ground black pepper
1 can (10 oz) white kidney beans (dried and rinsed)
1 package (9 oz) frozen Italian green beans, thawed

1 zucchini, cut into 1/2 inch chunks
1/2 cup medium shell pasta
2 tablespoons chopped parsley
grated parmesan cheese

In a large saucepan, heat the oil over medium heat. Add the celery, carrot, onion, garlic, and cabbage and cook, stirring frequently, until the vegetables are lightly browned. Add the **Coca-Cola®**, water, tomatoes, bouillon cubes, salt, basil, and pepper and heat to boiling. Reduce the heat to low. Add the remaining vegetables and shell pasta. Cover and simmer about 30 minutes or until the vegetables are tender.

Serve with chopped parsley and parmesan cheese sprinkled on top.

Swedish Fruit Soup

1 package (8 ounce) mixed dried fruits,
     cut in bite size pieces
1 1/2 cups water
1 cup **Coca-Cola®**
1/2 teaspoon ground cinnamon
1 package (3 ounce) cherry gelatin
3 cups **Minute Maid®** orange juice
sour cream

In a large saucepan, combine the dried fruit, water, **Coca-Cola®** and cinnamon. Bring to a boil, cover, reduce heat and simmer for 20 minutes.

Remove from the heat and add the gelatin, stirring until dissolved. Add the orange juice and chill.

Serve this soup cold, topped with sour cream.

Cold Orange Soup

1 envelope unflavored gelatin
1/4 cup hot water
1/4 cup **Sprite®**
2 cups **Minute Maid®** orange juice
1/4 cup lemon juice
1 tablespoon lime juice
1/4 cup sugar or honey
1 cup orange sections, diced
fresh mint sprigs

Dissolve the gelatin in the hot water. Add the **Sprite®**, fruit juices, and sugar. Chill for several hours. Just before serving, add the orange sections. Garnish with sprigs of mint.

Raspberry Fruit Soup

2 tablespoons quick-cooking tapioca
1/4 cup sugar
1/8 teaspoon salt

1/2 cup **Sprite®**
2 packages (10 ounce size) frozen raspberries,
        thawed, undrained
1/3 cup lemon juice
1 tablespoon butter or margarine
1/2 cup whipping cream or sour cream
ground nutmeg

In a saucepan, combine the tapioca, sugar, salt, **Sprite®**, and 1 package of the raspberries. Cook, stirring constantly, over medium heat until mixture boils. Reduce the heat and simmer uncovered for 5 minutes. Add the lemon juice and butter and let cool for 20 minutes.

Add the remaining package of raspberries, stirring to blend well. Chill. Serve in sherbet glasses. Top each with a dollop of whipped or sour cream and dust with nutmeg.

Lobster and Crab Bisque

1 can (4 ounce) crab meat, flaked
1 can (4 ounce) lobster, cut in small pieces
1 small onion, minced
2 tablespoons butter
2 tablespoons flour
1 teaspoon salt
dash of pepper
1/8 teaspoon celery salt
1 cup **Sprite®**
3 cups milk

Drain the crab meat and lobster and reserve the liquid. In a 2 quart saucepan, melt the butter and saute the onion until transparent. Stir in the flour, salt, pepper and celery salt. Cook, stirring constantly, until well blended and bubbling.

Remove from the heat and gradually stir in the **Sprite®** and milk. Bring to boil and boil for 1 minute, stirring constantly.

Stir in the lobster and crab meat. Add the reserved liquid and heat to serving temperature.

Serve with saltines or oyster crackers.

Anyone for a Dagwood? Our young host wheels out the makings for this heroic sandwich, then everyone builds his own. You begin with a French loaf, split almost in half lengthwise, and anything or everything goes in—chicken, ham, salami, cheese, green bell pepper, onion, tomato—you name it. Some people call them Submarines. Others refer to them as Poor Boys, Gondolas, Italian heroes, or Grinders, but everybody calls them wonderful— especially when teamed with frosty Coke.

An illustration and serving tip from the Winter 1956 issue of *Pause for Living*, a wonderful little magazine full of recipes, decorating tips, and much more. It was published for decades and distributed by **Coca-Cola®** bottlers.

CHAPTER 8

SALADS

There are many different kinds of salad. In this book we look mostly at the salads in which gelatin is an ingredient. These salads are cool and refreshing treats on hot summer days. Use a salad to bring back flagging appetites or as a light meal itself. Try **Coca-Cola®** Salad below—with **Coca-Cola®** and pecans, it's about as Southern as you can get this side of Atlanta, Georgia. Good!

Coca-Cola® Salad

3 ounce package cherry gelatin
3 ounce pkg strawberry gelatin
16 oz dark Bing cherries, pitted
20 ounce can crushed pineapple
8 ounces cream cheese
12 ounces **Coca-Cola®**
1 cup chopped pecans

Drain the cherries and pineapple, reserving juice. Heat the juice and dissolve the gelatin in it. Cut the cream cheese into very small chunks and add to the gelatin mixture. Add the cherries, pineapple, **Coca-Cola®** and pecans. Pour into a mold and chill.

Ambrosia Mold

1 pkg (3 ounces) orange-pineapple
flavored gelatin
1 cup boiling water
3/4 cup **Sprite®**
2/3 cup flaked coconut
2 oranges, peeled and sectioned
1 1/4 cups seedless grapes, halved
1 cup whipping cream, whipped

Dissolve the gelatin in boiling water and stir in the **Sprite®**. Chill until partially set. Stir in the oranges, grapes, and coconut and fold in the whipped cream. Pour into a lightly oiled 6 cup mold. Chill until set.

Heavenly Orange Salad

1 envelope unflavored gelatin
2 tablespoons cold water
1 package (6 ounces) orange Jell-O
2 cups boiling water
1 can (6 ounces) **Minute Maid®** orange juice concentrate
2 cans (13 ounces) Mandarin oranges, drained and cut up
1 can (15-1/4 ounces) crushed pineapple

Stir the unflavored gelatin into cold water. Add the orange Jell-O to boiling water. Stir in the unflavored gelatin mixture and blend until dissolved. Stir in the juice concentrate and add the mandarin oranges and pineapple. Pour into a dish or mold and congeal.

Topping:

1 package instant lemon pudding
1/2 cup **Fresca®**
1/4 cup powdered milk
1/2 pint Cool Whip

Mix the pudding, **Fresca®** and powdered milk until smooth. Fold in the Cool Whip. Spread the topping on the salad after it congeals.

Raspberry Salad

> 2 small packages raspberry Jell-O
> 1 1/2 cups hot water
> 2 cups **Minute Maid®** orange juice
> 1 jar cranberry-orange relish
> 1 small can crushed pineapple
> 1/2 cup nuts, chopped (optional)

Dissolve the Jell-O in hot water and add the orange juice. Chill until the mixture begins to set.

Stir in the relish, pineapple, and nuts. Chill.

Jell-O-Delite Salad

> 1 package (6 ounces) lime flavored gelatin
> 2 cups boiling water
> 2 cups **Sprite®**
> 2 cups miniature marshmallows
> 3 bananas, sliced
> 1 medium can crushed pineapple, drained (reserve juice)

Topping:

> 2 eggs
> 2 tablespoons flour
> 1/2 cup sugar
> 1 cup pineapple juice (reserved above)
> 1 package dry whipped topping mix
> 2 tablespoons butter

Dissolve the gelatin in boiling water and cool slightly. Drain the pineapple, reserving the juice. Add the **Sprite®**, marshmallows, bananas, and drained pineapple to the gelatin. Refrigerate.

Topping: Mix the eggs, sugar, and flour. Add enough water to the reserved juice to make 1 cup of liquid. Stir in the butter and juice. Cook over medium heat until thick, stirring often. Cool. Prepare the whipped topping mix according to package directions and fold into cooled cooked mixture.

When ready to serve, top the gelatin with the sauce.

Crab Salad

1 pound crab meat
1 medium onion, chopped
1/2 cup salad oil
1/3 cup cider vinegar
1/3 cup **Fresca®**

In a bowl, arrange the crab meat and onion in layers. Combine the remaining ingredients and pour over the top. Cover and refrigerate overnight. To serve, remove from bowl with a slotted spoon.

Georgia Shrimp Salad

2 cans frozen grapefruit sections, thawed and drained
1 package (3 ounces) cream cheese, softened
1/3 cup mayonnaise
1/4 cup **Coca-Cola®**
1/4 cup cocktail sauce
1/2 cup chopped pecans
2 tablespoons onion, minced
1 1/2 pounds shrimp, cleaned and cooked
lettuce cups

Blend the cream cheese and mayonnaise together until smooth. Add the **Coca-Cola®**, cocktail sauce, pecans and onion and mix thoroughly. Stir in the shrimp.

Place lettuce cups on salad plates and arrange the grapefruit in the cups. Spoon the shrimp mixture on top.

Tomato Salad

1 tablespoon salt
1/2 cup sugar
1-1/2 teaspoons pepper
1 teaspoon dry mustard
1/2 cup vinegar
1 medium onion, chopped
1/4 cup **Coca-Cola®**
1/4 cup catsup

1 cup salad oil
1 head lettuce, shredded
4 tomatoes, cut in wedges

Combine all of the ingredients, except the lettuce and tomato in blender and blend until smooth. Arrange the lettuce on salad plates and place the tomato wedges on the lettuce. Serve with the dressing. Note: the dressing may be blended and refrigerated, covered, for several hours.

Congealed Vegetable Salad

1 package orange gelatin
1 cup hot water
1 cup **Sprite®**
1/2 teaspoon salt
1 cup shredded carrots
1 cup diced green onions
1 cup diced celery

Dissolve the gelatin in the hot water, then add the **Sprite®**. Chill until partially set, then fold in the remaining ingredients. Pour the mixture into an oiled 1 1/2 quart mold and chill until firm.

Mixed Vegetable Salad

1 package (24 ounces) frozen mixed vegetables
1/4 cup scallions, chopped, including tops
1/4 cup green pepper, chopped
1/2 cup mayonnaise
1/4 cup **Fresca®**
salt and pepper to taste

In a small bowl, thoroughly mix the mayonnaise and **Fresca®**. Set aside. Cook the mixed vegetables according to the package directions and drain. Add the scallions and green pepper and cool.

Add the dressing, salt and pepper.

Store in the refrigerator until ready to use. Garnish with tomato wedges, if desired.

Out of This World Salad

1 package lemon Jell-O
1 cup hot water
8 ounces cream cheese, softened
1 small can crushed pineapple
1 teaspoon sugar
1 teaspoon vanilla
1/2 cup pecans
1 cup **Sprite®**

Dissolve the Jell-O in the hot water. Add the cream cheese, and stir until mixed. Let cool and add the pineapple, sugar, vanilla and pecans. Stir. Add the **Sprite®**, stir well, and chill until set.

CHAPTER 9
BREADS

Man (nor woman either, for that matter), as the old cliche goes, does not live by bread alone. Still, meals sure would be bland without crusty, flavorful morsels of bread, and that's what we offer you here. Enjoy.

Cranberry Bread

2 cups sifted flour
1/2 teaspoon salt
1 1/2 teaspoons baking powder
1/2 teaspoon soda
1 cup sugar
1 egg, beaten
2 tablespoons butter, melted
1/2 cup **Minute Maid®** orange juice
2 tablespoons hot water
1/2 cup pecans
1 cup whole cranberries
1 tablespoon orange rind, grated

Pierce cranberries so they won't burst. Combine the flour, salt, baking powder, soda and sugar. Add the egg, butter, orange juice and water. Mix well. Stir in the pecans, cranberries, and orange rind. Bake in a greased loaf pan for 1 hour and 10 minutes at 350 degrees.

Waffles

2 cups biscuit mix
1 egg
1/2 cup cooking oil
1 1/3 cups **Sprite®**

Mix all ingredients together well, then pour batter onto a hot waffle iron, or onto a hot griddle for pancakes. Watch carefully—they don't take long to cook.

Note: Batter does not store well. But cooked waffles can be reheated in toaster or microwave.

Ambrosia Muffins

1 egg, beaten
1/2 cup milk
1/3 cup cooking oil
1/4 cup **Minute Maid®** orange juice concentrate
1 3/4 cups all purpose flour
2 tablespoons sugar
2 1/2 teaspoons baking powder
3/4 teaspoon salt
1/2 cup flaked coconut

Grease 10 muffin cups and set aside. In a bowl, combine the egg, milk, oil, and juice concentrate. In a separate bowl, thoroughly stir together the flour, sugar, baking powder and salt. Add the egg mixture all at once, stirring just until moistened. Fold in the coconut. Fill the prepared cups 2/3 full. Bake for about 20 minutes at 375 degrees. Remove the muffins from the pans. If desired, lightly brush the tops with additional juice concentrate and sprinkle generously with additional sugar.

Date-Nut Bread

1 package (8 ounces) pitted dates, chopped
1 1/4 cups **Coca-Cola®**
1 cup firmly packed light brown sugar or granulated sugar
2 tablespoons oil

2 cups all-purpose flour
1 teaspoon baking powder
1 teaspoon soda
1 egg, well beaten
1 teaspoon vanilla extract
1/2 cup chopped pecans or walnuts

Heat the **Coca-Cola®** to boiling. Remove from heat and stir in the dates, mixing very well. Stir in the sugar and oil. Let cool while preparing the other ingredients. Stir together the flour, baking powder and soda. Add to the dates, mixing thoroughly.

Stir in the egg, vanilla and nuts. Pour into a greased and floured 9x5x3-inch loaf pan. Bake at 350 degrees for about 1 hour or until a toothpick inserted in the center comes out clean.

Cool in the pan on a rack for 20 minutes. Remove the loaf from the pan and set it on the rack, top side up. When cold, wrap and store overnight before slicing.

Note: Great with cream cheese

Sweet Potato Biscuits

2 cups self-rising flour
1/8 teaspoon salt
1/3 cup shortening
1 cup cooked mashed sweet potatoes
1/3 cup **Sprite®**
1 tablespoon powdered milk

Preheat oven to 400 degrees. Grease a cookie sheet. Sprinkle salt on the potatoes. Sift the flour with the powdered milk.

Cut the shortening and potatoes into the flour. Add the **Sprite®** gradually (more or less according to potatoes).

Mix well and roll out. Cut with biscuit cutter or shape with hands. Bake on greased pan for 12 to 15 minutes in preheated oven.

Butter and serve hot

Date Nut Loaf

1 package pitted dates, chopped
1 cup boiling water
1/2 cup **Sprite®**
1/2 cup butter
1 1/2 cups sugar
1 teaspoon salt
2 eggs, beaten
3 cups flour
1 teaspoon baking soda
1 teaspoon cream of tartar
1 teaspoon vanilla
1 cup nuts, chopped

Sift together the flour, baking soda and cream of tartar and set aside. Place the dates in a large bowl and add the water, **Sprite®**, butter, sugar and salt. Set aside until cool. Add the eggs to the dates and mix. Add the flour mixture and mix well. Stir in the vanilla and nuts. Pour into a greased and floured loaf pan. Bake at 325 degrees for 1 hour.

Orange Date Bread

1 stick margarine
1/4 cup sugar
1/2 cup light brown sugar
2 eggs, beaten
1 tablespoon grated orange peel
1/2 teaspoon vanilla
1/2 cup sour milk
1/2 cup Minute Maid orange juice
3 cups sifted flour
2 teaspoons baking powder
1/2 teaspoon soda
1/2 teaspoon salt
1 cup dates, chopped
1 cup nuts, chopped

In a mixing bowl, cream together the margarine and sugars. Add the eggs, orange peel and vanilla and beat until light and fluffy. Add the sour milk and beat well. Add the orange juice and beat thoroughly. Sift together the flour, baking powder, soda and salt. Add to the creamed mixture and stir just until blended.

Fold in the dates and nuts and pour into a greased 9x5x3 inch loaf pan. Bake at 350 degrees for 1 hour to 1 hour and 10 minutes.

Remove from pan and cool before slicing.

Pumpkin Bread

> 3 cups sugar
> 4 eggs, beaten
> 1 cup salad oil
> 1-1/2 teaspoons salt
> 1 teaspoon cinnamon
> 1 teaspoon nutmeg
> 2/3 cup **Coca-Cola®**
> 2 cups canned pumpkin
> 3-1/2 cups flour
> 2 teaspoons soda

In a large bowl, mix the sugar, eggs, oil, salt, cinnamon, nutmeg and **Coca-Cola®**. Add the pumpkin and mix well. Stir in the flour and soda. Place in 2 well greased loaf pans. Bake at 350 degrees for 1 hour.

Easy Cheese Muffins

> 1 cup sifted self-rising flour
> 1 cup self-rising cornmeal
> 2/3 cup grated cheese
> 1 cup **Sprite®**
> 1/3 cup powdered milk
> 1 egg, beaten
> 2 tablespoons shortening, melted

Combine the flour, cornmeal, and powdered milk in a bowl and add the cheese.

Combine the **Sprite®**, egg and shortening. Add to the cheese mixture and blend thoroughly. Place in hot, greased muffin cups and bake at 425 degrees for about 20 minutes.

The Autumn 1958 issue of *Pause for Living*—that fascinating little magazine sent out for decades by **Coca-Cola®** bottlers—featured this use of bread in its serving tips.

112   BREADS

CHAPTER 10
FRUITS

Ever since Eve gave Adam that apple, we've all pretty well liked fruit. You'll be pleasantly surprised at how products such as **Coca-Cola®** and **Fresca®** enhance the flavors of fresh fruit. Also, the recipes in this chapter are easy and quick to prepare.

Coca-Cola® Fruit Delight

1 can (16 ounces) sliced peaches
1 package (3 ounces)
    cherry flavored gelatin
1 package (3 ounces)
    raspberry flavored gelatin
1 1/2 cups boiling water
1 1/2 cups **Coca-Cola®**
1 can (16 oz) sliced pears, drained
1/2 cup sour cream
1/2 cup mayonnaise

Drain the peaches, reserving the syrup. In a mixing bowl, dissolve the gelatins in the boiling water. Add the **Coca-Cola®** and the reserved syrup. Chill until partially set. Fold in the pears and peaches. Pour into a 6 cup mold and chill until firm. Combine the sour cream and mayonnaise and serve as a topping.

Coca-Cola® Fruit Cup

pineapple
orange
grapefruit
sweet cherries
Coca-Cola®
mint cherries

Cut the pineapple, orange and grapefruit into small cubes. Fill sherbert glasses with the fruit. Add a few cherries. Pour **Coca-Cola®** over to cover. Top with green mint cherries for contrast.

Hot Fruit with Cranberry Sauce

2 cans purple plums
1 can pineapple chunks
1 jar maraschino cherries
1 can cranberry sauce
1 can pears
1 can apricot halves
2 to 3 sliced bananas
1/2 cup **Coca-Cola®**

Drain the fruits well, remove the pits and cut into bite-size pieces. Mix all the fruits together. Grease a long oblong pan or glass casserole dish. Place the fruit mixture into the casserole dish and slice the cranberry sauce over the fruit. Pour the **Coca-Cola®** over the fruit and sauce. Bake at 350 degrees for 45 minutes.

Note: Almost any canned fruit may be used and bananas may be left out.

Poached Summer Fruit

1 cup **Minute Maid®** orange juice
1 cup sugar
julienne peel of one lemon
juice of one lemon
1 pound small plums, pitted and quartered
1 can (16 ounces) peach halves, drained

1 can (17 ounces) unpeeled apricot halves, drained
sprigs of mint

In a saucepan, combine the orange juice, sugar, lemon peel and juice. Cook at a full rolling boil until it becomes a thick syrup. Reduce the heat, add the plums and simmer for 5 minutes. Add the peaches and apricots and simmer for 2 additional minutes. With a slotted spoon, place the fruit in a serving bowl. Bring the syrup to a boil again and remove it from the heat. Add the mint to the syrup and pour over the fruit. Chill.

Hot Fruit Salad

1 medium can peach halves
1 medium can pear halves
1 medium can apricot halves
1 medium can pineapple slices
1 medium can apple rings
1 medium can maraschino cherries, halved
2 tablespoons cornstarch
1 cup brown sugar
1 cup **Sprite®**

Drain the fruit, reserving the liquid. Arrange the fruit in a large baking dish. In a small pan or the top of a double boiler, to the liquid add the cornstarch, sugar and **Sprite®**. Cook over hot water, stirring constantly, until thick. Pour the mixture over the fruit. Bake at 350 degrees for 30 minutes. May be refrigerated for several days.

Fruit Medley

5 cups of mixed fruit, cut in bite size pieces
(apples, grapes, blueberries, bananas,
and strawberries work well)
1 cup plain low-fat yogurt
1/4 cup wheat germ
1 cup **Fresca®**

In a small bowl, mix the yogurt with the wheat germ and add the **Fresca®**. Place the fruit in a large bowl and add the yogurt mixture. Stir well. Refrigerate for several hours before serving.

Harvest Fruit Compote

1 can (15 1/4 ounces) pineapple chunks
1 package (12 ounces) pitted, dried prunes
1 cup dried apricots
2 cups water
1 can (21 ounces) cherry pie filling
3/4 cup **Coca-Cola®**
3/4 teaspoon cardamom

In a 3-quart casserole dish, place the undrained pineapple, prunes, and apricots. In a bowl, combine the water, **Coca-Cola®**, cherry pie filling, and cardamom and pour it over the fruit.

Cover and bake in a 350 degree oven for 1 1/2 hours. Serve warm or cold.

Whipped Fruit

2 cans (16 ounces each) fruit cocktail
1 cup **Minute Maid®** orange juice
1 package (3 ounce) orange or lemon flavored gelatin
peel of one lemon, grated
2 tablespoons lemon juice
1 teaspoon vanilla extract
2 egg whites (room temperature)

Drain the fruit cocktail, reserving 2/3 cup of liquid. In a saucepan, combine 1/2 cup of the orange juice with the reserved liquid and heat to boiling. Add the gelatin and dissolve completely.

Stir in the remaining orange juice, lemon peel, lemon juice, and vanilla. Chill approximately 1 hour, until partially set. Add the egg whites and beat with an electric mixer about 8 to 10 minutes, until it has doubled in size and reached a creamy consistency.

In a serving bowl, spread half the fruit cocktail and top with the gelatin mixture. Chill until firm and top with the remaining fruit.

Baked Apples

4 large baking apples
1/4 cup packed brown sugar
1/4 teaspoon ground nutmeg
4 teaspoons butter or margarine
1 cup **Coca-Cola®**
1/2 cup dairy sour cream (optional)
ground nutmeg (optional)

Remove and discard the core of the apples. Peel a strip from the top of each apple. Place the apples in an 8x8x2 inch baking dish. In a bowl, stir together the brown sugar, and the 1/4 teaspoon nutmeg. Spoon the sugar mixture into the apple centers.

Top each apple with 1 teaspoon of the butter. Pour the **Coca-Cola®** into the baking dish. Bake in a 350 degree oven about 1 hour or until the apples are tender, basting with **Coca-Cola®** occasionally.

Serve warm , topped with a dollop of sour cream and a dash of nutmeg, if desired.

Grapefruit Sections in Coca-Cola®

grapefruit
Coca-Cola®

Peel ripe grapefruit, removing the white pith. Separate the sections and place in sherbert dishes and chill. Pour ice-cold **Coca-Cola®** over to cover. (1 grapefruit and a 6 ounce bottle of **Coca-Cola®** yields 3 to 4 servings.)

Grapefruit with Coca-Cola®

grapefruit
powdered sugar
Coca-Cola®

Cut grapefruit in half and remove the centers. Loosen the pulp from the skin and membranes with a sharp knife. Sprinkle 1 tablespoon of powdered sugar over each half of the grapefruit. Chill for 1 hour. Before serving, fill the center of the grapefruit with **Coca-Cola®**.

Figs with Honey and Cream

1 quart fresh figs, stems removed
1 pint **Coca-Cola®**
1/3 cup honey
1 pint heavy cream

Wash the figs and place them in a saucepan. Mix the **Coca-Cola®** and honey and pour it over the figs. Bring the mixture to a boil and reduce the heat.

Simmer for 5 minutes and chill. Serve with cream.

Mixed Fruit

5 egg yolks
1 cup sugar
1 cup cream
1 cup powdered sugar
1/2 cup **Coca-Cola®**
3 pints fresh fruit cubes

Put the egg yolks in the top of a double boiler, stir in the sugar, cream and powdered sugar. Cook over hot water until slightly thickened. Add the **Coca-Cola®**, stirring to blend, then cool. Place the fruit in a large serving bowl and pour the sauce over the fruit.

Snowcap Strawberries

2 pints fresh strawberries
1 egg white
2/3 cup sugar
1/4 cup **Sprite®**
1 1/2 teaspoons white corn syrup
1/4 teaspoon salt
1/2 teaspoon vanilla

Wash and drain the strawberries and set aside. In the top of a double boiler, combine the egg white, sugar, **Sprite®**, syrup, and salt. Blend with an electric mixer. Place over rapidly boiling water and beat at high speed until the mixture forms peaks when the beater is raised. Remove from heat and add the vanilla.

Beat until thick and of a spreading consistency and remove from over the water. Hold each strawberry by the stem end and dip into the mixture to coat. Place on wax paper and let stand at room temperature until coating is set.

Strawberry Snowball Salad

1 cup boiling water
1 package (3 ounces) strawberry flavored gelatin
3/4 cup **Sprite®**
1 package (3 ounces) cream cheese, softened
1/3 cup nuts, chopped fine
1 tablespoon sugar
2 cups fresh strawberries

In a bowl, pour the boiling water over the gelatin, stirring until the gelatin is dissolved. Stir in the **Sprite®**. Chill until slightly thickened but not set.

Shape the cream cheese into 18 balls and roll each in nuts. Sprinkle the sugar over the strawberries and mix gently.

Pour 1/3 cup of the thickened gelatin into a 6-cup ring mold. Arrange the cheese balls evenly in the gelatin. Spoon the sweetened strawberries over the cheese balls and gelatin. Pour the remaining thickened gelatin carefully over the berries. Chill until firm. If desired, garnish with strawberries.

Summer Fruit Bowl

2 cups watermelon balls
2 red unpeeled apples, cut in thin wedges
1 cantaloupe, sliced in wedges
2 cups grapefruit sections
2 bananas, sliced diagonally
1 can (6 ounce) **Minute Maid®** orange juice concentrate

Place the watermelon balls in the center of a large serving bowl. Arrange the remaining fruit around the watermelon.

Spoon the orange juice over the fruit. Serve chilled.

Bonus: Elephants and Penguins

While perusing old issues of *Pause for Living*—the wonderful quarterly magazine published for distribution by **Coca-Cola®** bottlers years ago—we found instructions for making these little elephants and penguins. They are just too cute to allow this knowledge to sink into obscurity, so we republish the instructions here in the hopes of preserving our little friends for another few decades.

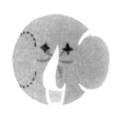

(from the Summer 1955 *Pause for Living*)...

These mirth-provoking little animals serve many a purpose in addition to that of party favor. Junior in bed with the sniffles? Perk up his breakfast tray with an orange looking more like an elephant. Our penguin looks so much like his live counterpart in the Arctics that you almost expect him to waddle. He has appeal for the young-at-heart of any age. That makes him a whimsical decoration for any relish tray or salad plate.

The Elephant

Cut through the skin of an orange, as shown (top left of this page), to form the elephant's trunk, making its length a little more than one quarter the total circumference of the orange. Curve the trunk back toward the stem end of the orange, working it carefully over your fingers to prevent it from breaking. If necessary, pare off more of the inner skin where the trunk curves. Fasten in position with a bit of toothpick.

Place cloves in position for eyes. At each side, cut the skin loose for ears, tracing an outline with a toothpick first if you feel unsure of your skill with the paring knife. Insert a short length of toothpick between ears and body to hold ears in a forward position.

Attach four large gumdrops to the body with toothpicks to form sturdy legs. Place a long narrow gumdrop in the elephant's trunk. Split one of the long gumdrops in half lengthwise and attach one of the halves for a tail.

The Penguin

The trick to producing smooth white hardboiled eggs for the body is this: Put the eggs in boiling water and cook for 12 minutes. Place immediately in cold water to make it easy to remove the shells. Now the shells may be removed at your convenience. Cut a small slice from the large end of an egg and attach with two toothpick halves to the carrot feet, shaped as shown in the bottom drawing at the start of this section.

Cut a large ripe olive in half, remove the stone and attach olive halves to each side of the body for wings. The head is a ripe olive attached with a whole toothpick for security. A slim sliver of carrot forms the nose, with bits of toothpicks for eyes. Add cloves down the front for buttons.

CHAPTER 11

DESSERTS

T his, of course, is our coauthor's *favorite* section! The yummy desserts here immediately got his attention, and he unselfishly volunteered to help with the taste testing. We think he may be gaining a little weight, though. Still, as he agrees, it's for a good cause. He's really that kind of guy.

CAKES

Sprite® Cake

2 sticks butter or margarine
1/2 cup shortening
3 cups sugar
5 eggs
3 cups plain flour
1 teaspoon vanilla flavoring
2 teaspoons lemon flavoring
12 ounces **Sprite®**

Cream the butter, shortening and sugar well; add the eggs and flour gradually. Add the vanilla and lemon flavorings and slowly add the **Sprite®**. Bake in a tube pan for 1 hour and 10 minutes at 325 degrees.

Coca-Cola® Cake

2 cups unsifted plain flour
1 cup sugar
2 sticks butter or margarine
3 tablespoons cocoa
1 cup **Coca-Cola®**
1/2 cup buttermilk
2 eggs, beaten
1 teaspoon baking soda
1 teaspoon vanilla
1 1/2 cups miniature marshmallows

Sift the flour and sugar into a large mixing bowl. In a saucepan, heat the butter, cocoa, and **Coca-Cola®** until they boil. Pour this over the flour and sugar mixture, then mix thoroughly. Add the buttermilk, eggs, soda, vanilla and marshmallows and mix well. The batter will be thin and the marshmallows will come to the top. Bake at 350 degrees in a sheet pan (2x12x14 inches) for 30 to 35 minutes.

Icing:

1 stick butter or margarine, melted
3 tablespoons cocoa
6 or 7 tablespoons **Coca-Cola®**
1 box confectioners' sugar

Pour the first three ingredients over the confectioners' sugar and mix well. Pour this over the cake while it is warm. Optional: Add one cup toasted chopped pecans to icing.

Coca-Cola® Chocolate Cake

4 cups plain flour
8 tablespoons cocoa
3 teaspoons cinnamon
1 teaspoon salt
2 teaspoons soda
4 cups sugar
1 pound butter
4 eggs
1 cup buttermilk
4 teaspoons vanilla
2 cups **Coca-Cola®**

Icing:

> 1/2 cup butter
> 1/2 cup **Coca-Cola®**
> 6 tablespoons cocoa
> 1 cup chopped pecans
> 2 teaspoons vanilla
> 2 boxes powdered sugar

Grease and flour an 11x17 inch pan. Sift together the dry ingredients and set aside. In a saucepan, heat the butter and **Coca-Cola®** until the butter melts. Add the eggs, vanilla, and buttermilk and mix well. Add the liquid to the dry ingredients and beat until smooth. The batter will be very thin. Pour into the prepared pan and bake at 350 degrees for 30 minutes. (Will fill 2 tube pans or 2 paper-lined cupcake tins. Bake tube cakes for 60 minutes; cupcakes for 15 minutes.) This cake must be iced while warm.

Icing: In a saucepan, heat the butter and **Coca-Cola®**. Do not boil. Add all of the remaining ingredients and mix well. Pour over cake.

Coca-Cola® and Walnut Cake

> 3/4 pound butter or margarine, softened
> 2 1/2 cups sugar
> 5 eggs
> 3 cups all-purpose flour
> 1/3 cup cocoa
> 1/2 teaspoon baking soda
> 1/8 teaspoon salt
> 1/2 cup buttermilk
> 1/2 cup **Coca-Cola®**
> 1 cup chopped walnuts

Preheat the oven to 350 degrees. Grease and lightly flour a 12-cup bundt pan or a 10-inch tube pan. In a large mixing bowl, cream together the butter and sugar. Add the eggs one at a time, beating well after each addition. In a medium bowl, combine the flour, cocoa, baking soda, and salt and stir to mix. Add to the egg mixture alternately with the buttermilk and **Coca-Cola®**. Stir in the walnuts. Pour into the prepared pan. Bake for 50 to 60 minutes, or until a wooden pick inserted near the center of the cake comes out clean. Remove cake from the pan immediately.

Pineapple Sprite® Cake

1 box pineapple cake mix
1 box instant vanilla or lemon pudding
3/4 cup oil
10 ounces **Sprite**®
6 eggs
1 1/2 cups sugar
11 ounces crushed pineapple
3/4 stick margarine
2 tablespoons flour
1 cup coconut (optional)

In a large mixing bowl, combine the cake mix, pudding mix, oil and **Sprite**® and mix well. Add 4 eggs one at a time, beating well after each addition. Pour into a 9x13 inch pan and bake at 350 degrees for 30 to 40 minutes. Make a topping by combining the sugar, remaining eggs, undrained pineapple, margarine and flour. Cook until thick, stirring constantly. Stir in the coconut and spread on the hot cake.

Mello Yello® Cake

1 1/2 cups Crisco
3 cups plain flour
1 cup **Mello Yello**®
1 teaspoon vanilla
1 teaspoon lemon
3 cups sugar
5 eggs

Let the eggs and **Mello Yello**® sit out long enough to reach room temperature. Preheat the oven to 325 degrees. In a large mixing bowl, cream together the shortening and sugar until light and fluffy. Add the eggs, one at a time, beating well after each addition. Add the flour and **Mello Yello**® alternately starting and ending with the flour. Add the flavorings. Bake at 325 degrees for 1 1/2 hours.

Pineapple Cake

1 package yellow cake mix, prepared
15 1/2 ounces crushed pineapple
1 package vanilla pudding mix

1 cup **Fresca**®
1/3 cup powdered milk
whipped cream

Prepare the cake according to the package directions in a 13x9x2 inch pan. While the cake is still hot from the oven, pour the undrained pineapple over the cake in the pan. Refrigerate overnight. Combine the pudding mix, powdered milk and **Fresca**® and let set for 5 minutes. Spread the pudding over the cake. Just before serving, spread a layer of whipped cream on top.

Coconut Pound Cake

2 sticks butter or margarine
2/3 cup   shortening
2 1/2 cups sugar
5 eggs
3 cups cake flour
1/3 cup powdered milk
1 cup **Sprite**®
1 can flaked coconut
1 teaspoon coconut flavoring
1 teaspoon vanilla flavoring

Mix the ingredients in the order given and bake in a tube pan at 325 degrees for 1 1/2 hours.

Coconut Cake

1 package yellow cake mix
1 package vanilla instant pudding
1 3/4 cups **Sprite**®
4 eggs
1/4 cup oil
2 cups coconut
1 cup chopped pecans

Grease and flour 2 layer cake pans. In a large mixing bowl, blend the cake mix, pudding mix, **Sprite**®, eggs and oil. Beat at high speed for 4 minutes. Stir in the coconut and pecans and pour into the pans. Bake at 350 degrees for 35 minutes. Cool and frost.

Family Gathering Cake

1 package lemon cake mix
1 large package instant vanilla pudding mix
2 cups **Fresca®**
2/3 cup powdered milk
1 large container Cool Whip
1 package frozen coconut
1 large can crushed pineapple with juice
3/4 to 1 cup sugar

Prepare the cake according to the package directions, baking it in a 9x13-inch pan. In a saucepan, mix the pineapple and sugar, heating until boiling, stirring frequently. Boil for 4 minutes. Mix the vanilla pudding with the **Fresca®** and powdered milk. Top the cake in the following order: the pineapple and sugar mixture, the vanilla pudding mixture, the Cool Whip, and the coconut. For special occasions, you may want to use food coloring to tint the coconut.

Hawaiian Wedding Cake

1 yellow cake mix
2 eggs
small can crushed pineapple
8 ounces cream cheese, softened
1 small package vanilla instant pudding
1 cup **Fresca®**
1/3 cup powdered milk
8 ounces Cool Whip
1/2 cup coconut

Drain the juice from the pineapple and add water to make 1 1/2 cups of liquid. Combine the liquid with the cake mix and eggs. Bake according to the directions on the box for an 11x13 inch cake. When the cake is cooled, combine the cream cheese, pudding mix, **Fresca®**, and milk and mix well. Spread the cream cheese mixture on the cake. Mix together the pineapple and Cool Whip and spread it on the cake. Top the cake with coconut. Refrigerate until ready to serve.

Orange Layer Cake

1 box orange cake mix
1 box (3 ounces) orange Jell-O
1 cup **Sprite®**

1/2 cup oil
2 eggs
16 ounces sour cream
1 1/2 cups sugar
3 to 4 tablespoons orange juice with pulp
12 ounces coconut
8 ounces Cool Whip

Grease and flour three eight inch layer pans. Combine the cake mix, orange Jell-O, **Sprite®**, oil and eggs, mix well and pour into the prepared pans. Bake at 350 degrees for 20 to 25 minutes. Let cool.

Cream together the sour cream, sugar, orange juice, and coconut. Reserve 1 cup of this mixture. Place the filling in the refrigerator to chill. Spread the chilled filling between the layers. Combine the Cool Whip with the reserved filling and whip. Ice the cake with the Cool Whip mixture.

This cake is excellent to prepare ahead and freeze.

Strawberry Date Cake

1 box strawberry cake mix
1 envelope Dream Whip
1 small package instant vanilla pudding
1/2 cup **Sprite®**
1 teaspoon strawberry flavoring
1/2 cup oil
10 ounce package strawberries
4 eggs
1/2 cup chopped sugared dates
1/2 cup coconut

In a large mixing bowl, combine all of the dry ingredients. Add the **Sprite®**, flavoring, oil and strawberries and mix at medium speed for 2 minutes. Add the eggs one at a time, beating well after each addition. Beat for 2 more minutes after adding the eggs.

Fold in the remaining ingredients and place in a large (12 cup) greased and floured bundt pan. Bake at 350 degrees for 45 to 55 minutes or until done.

Orange Raisin Cake

1 orange
1 cup raisins
1/3 cup walnuts
2 cups flour
1 teaspoon baking soda
1 teaspoon salt
3/4 cup sugar
1/3 cup powdered milk
1/2 cup shortening
1 cup **Sprite®**
2 eggs

Topping:

1/3 cup **Minute Maid®** orange juice
1/3 cup sugar
1 teaspoon cinnamon
1/4 cup walnuts, chopped

Grind together the entire orange with the raisins and walnuts. Sift together the flour, baking soda, salt, 3/4 cup sugar, and powdered milk. Add the shortening and 3/4 cup **Sprite®** and beat for 2 minutes. Add the eggs and remaining **Sprite®** and beat for another 2 minutes. Fold in the orange and raisin mixture. Pour into a well-greased and lightly-floured 9x13 inch pan. Bake for 40 to 50 minutes at 350 degrees.

Drip the orange juice over the warm cake. Combine 1/3 cup sugar, cinnamon and walnuts for topping and sprinkle over the warm cake.

Strawberry Banana Cake

1 box strawberry cake mix
4 heaping tablespoons butter recipe cake mix (Pillsbury)
1 package instant banana pudding
1 package Dream Whip
1 1/4 cups **Sprite®**
1/2 cup Crisco oil
1 teaspoon banana flavoring
4 eggs
1 medium or large banana, mashed to mushy state

Preheat the oven to 300 degrees. In a large mixing bowl, combine the dry ingredients. Add the **Sprite®**, oil and flavoring and mix well. Add the eggs one at a time, beating well after each addition. Add the banana and beat on high speed for 2 minutes. Pour into a well greased and floured bundt pan and bake at 300 degrees for 65 minutes.

Drizzle:

> 1 cup confectioners' sugar
> 1 1/2 tablespoons milk
> 2 teaspoons butter flavoring
> 1 teaspoon strawberry flavoring
> 1 drop red food coloring

In a mixing bowl, blend all of the ingredients together by hand. Drizzle the icing over the slightly warm or cold cake. Use more or less milk, depending on how thick you want the drizzle.

Butter Pecan-Banana Pudding Cake

> 1/2 cup mashed bananas
> 1 package yellow cake mix (2 layer size)
> 1 package butter pecan flavored
>   instant pudding and pie filling (4 serving size)
> 4 eggs
> 1 cup **Coca-Cola®**
> 1/4 cup oil
> 1/2 cup finely chopped nuts, optional

Glaze:

> 1 tablespoon hot milk or water
> 1 cup sifted powdered sugar

In a large mixing bowl, blend all of the ingredients. Beat for 4 minutes at medium speed. Pour into a greased and floured 10-inch bundt pan. Bake at 350 degrees for 50 minutes or until the cake springs back when lightly pressed and pulls away from sides. Do not under-bake. Cool in the pan for 15 minutes, remove and cool on a rack.

Glaze: Stir the hot milk into the powdered sugar and drizzle over the cake.

Walnut Banana Cake

1 1/2 boxes banana cake mix (half box is 2-1/4 cups)
3 3/4 ounce package instant banana pudding
3 3/4 ounce package instant French vanilla pudding
3/4 cup oil
1 cup pear nectar
1/2 cup **Sprite®**
6 eggs
2 medium to large bananas, mashed
1 cup walnuts, chopped

Preheat the oven to 325 degrees. In a large mixing bowl, blend the cake mix and puddings with the oil, nectar and **Sprite®** for 2 minutes at medium speed. Add the eggs one at a time, beating well after each addition. Add the bananas and beat at medium to high speed for 1 minute. Fold in the walnuts. Grease and flour a large tube pan and line the bottom with waxed paper. Pour the batter into the pan and bake for 1 hour and 15 minutes or until done.

Caramel Icing:

1/4 cup milk
1/2 cup light brown sugar
4 tablespoons butter or margarine
2 cups confectioners sugar
1 teaspoon vanilla
dash of salt

In a saucepan, heat the milk, brown sugar and butter and let them come to a boil over low heat, stirring constantly. Let boil for 1 minute. Remove from the heat. Add the confectioners sugar and beat until smooth. Add the vanilla and salt. Stir well and ice the warm cake. If the icing is too thick, add more milk. If you prefer a darker color, add 1 tablespoon dark brown sugar.

California Orchard Cake

1 box orange cake mix
1/2 box pineapple cake mix (2 1/4 cups)
1 small box peach gelatin
1 box pineapple instant pudding
3/4 cup oil

3/4 cup pear nectar
3/4 cup **Sprite®**
6 eggs
1 package Dream Whip

In a large mixing bowl, combine the cake mixes, gelatin, and pudding with the oil, nectar, and **Sprite®**. Add the eggs one at a time, beating well after each addition. Fold in the Dream Whip and mix well. Grease and flour a large tube pan and line the bottom with waxed paper. Pour the batter into the pan and bake at 325 degrees for 1 hour and 10 minutes or until done.

Icing:

1 pound confectioners' sugar
1 stick butter
1/4 cup milk
1/2 teaspoon orange flavoring
1/2 teaspoon coconut flavoring
1/2 cup coconut
1 drop red food coloring
1 drop yellow food coloring

Put the sugar in a mixing bowl and make a well. Pour the melted butter into the well and mix together, until it forms a ball. Add milk until it reaches a spreadable consistency. Then add the flavorings, coconut, and coloring to form an apricot color. Spread over the cake while it is still warm. Let the icing run down the sides while spreading with a knife.

Orange Pound Cake

2 cups plain flour
1 cup vegetable shortening
1 3/4 cups sugar
5 eggs
3/4 cup Minute Maid orange juice
1 teaspoon vanilla

Grease, flour and line with waxed paper, the bottom of a tube pan. Cream the sugar and shortening. Add the eggs one at a time, beating well after each addition. Sift the flour three times and add to the egg mixture alternately with the orange juice, starting and ending with the flour. Stir in the vanilla. Bake for one hour at 350 degrees. Use your favorite frosting.

Strawberry Cake

4 eggs
3/4 cup oil
3/4 cup **Sprite®**
1/2 cup frozen strawberries, thawed
1 box white cake mix
3 tablespoons cake flour
1 small box strawberry gelatin

Combine the cake mix, cake flour, and gelatin and set aside. In a large mixing bowl, combine the eggs, oil, **Sprite®** and strawberries. Add the combined dry ingredients and mix well. Bake in two 9 inch pans (lined with waxed paper) at 350 degrees for about 20 minutes or until the center springs back to the touch. Cool and ice.

Icing:

1 box confectioners' sugar
1 stick butter
1/2 cup strawberries
red food coloring (optional)

Combine all of the ingredients, adding enough strawberries to obtain a spreading consistency. If a deeper color is desired, add several drops of red food coloring. Decorate the top with fresh strawberries.

Cherry Date Cake

1 box cherry cake mix
1 package Dream Whip
1 box French vanilla instant pudding
1 cup **cherry Coke®**
1/2 cup oil
4 eggs
1/2 cup maraschino cherries, sliced
1/2 cup dates, chopped
1/2 cup coconut

In a large mixing bowl, combine the cake mix, Dream Whip, pudding mix, **cherry Coke®** and oil and beat for about 3 minutes. Add the eggs one at a time, beating well after each addition. Add the cherries, dates and coconut. Pour into a greased, floured bundt pan. Bake for 45 to 50 minutes at 350 degrees. Frost if desired. The icing on page 124 is good!

Raisin Cake

2 cups sugar
2 cups **Coca-Cola®**
1 package (16 ounces) raisins
1/2 pound butter
2 teaspoons baking powder
3 1/2 cups flour
1 teaspoon cinnamon
1 cup chopped walnuts
pinch of nutmeg

Boil the sugar, **Coca-Cola®**, raisins, and butter together for 5 minutes. Add the baking powder, flour, cinnamon, walnuts and nutmeg and stir well. Bake in a loaf pan at 350 degrees for 1 1/2 hour.

Dark Fruit Cake

1/2 pound butter
2 cups sugar
8 eggs
4 cups flour, sifted
1 teaspoon salt
1 teaspoon cinnamon
1 teaspoon nutmeg
1 cup **Minute Maid®** orange juice
1/2 pound raisins
1/2 pound currants
1/2 pound cherries
1/2 pound almonds
1/2 pound dates
1/2 pound pecans
1/2 pound pineapple
1/2 pound citron

Cream together the butter and sugar. Add the eggs and beat well. Sift 3 cups of flour with the salt, cinnamon and nutmeg. Add to the egg mixture alternately with the orange juice. Mix the fruits and nuts with the remaining cup of flour. Add the batter and mix well. Pour into metal pans, greased and floured and lined with waxed paper. Bake at 250 degrees for 2-1/2 hours or until done.

Pistachio Cake

1 box yellow cake mix
1 box pistachio instant pudding mix
1/2 cup oil
1/3 cup sugar
1 cup **Sprite®**
1 teaspoon vanilla
5 eggs
5 1/2 ounces chocolate syrup
1/2 cup nuts, chopped
1/2 cup semi-sweet chocolate chips

In a large mixing bowl, combine the cake mix, pudding mix, oil, sugar, **Sprite®**, vanilla and eggs, and beat well for 2 minutes. Combine 1 cup of the batter with the chocolate syrup. Grease and flour a bundt pan. Sprinkle the nuts and chocolate chips in the bottom of the pan. Pour the batter on top of the nuts and chips. Swirl the chocolate batter on top. Bake for 1 hour at 350 degrees. Cool for 10 minutes, then remove from pan.

Watergate Cake

1 box white cake mix
1 package pistachio instant pudding mix
3 eggs
1 cup **Sprite®**
1 cup Wesson oil
1/2 to 1 cup chopped nuts

In a large mixing bowl, combine all of the ingredients and beat together for 4 minutes. Bake in 2 layer pans (9 inch) at 350 degrees for 45 minutes.

Frosting:

1 package Dream Whip, dry
1 package pistachio instant pudding mix
1/3 cup powdered milk
1 cup **Fresca®**
4 1/2 ounces Cool Whip, thawed

Beat the first four ingredients until very firm and creamy. Fold in the Cool Whip.

Note: To increase the moisture content, bake cake 2 days ahead of time. Keep it refrigerated.

Frosted Lemon Cake

1 1/2 boxes lemon cake mix (half box is 2 1/4 cups)
1 box lemon instant pudding
3/4 cup oil
1 1/2 cups **Mello Yello®**
2 teaspoons lemon flavoring
1 teaspoon coconut flavoring
6 eggs
1 package Dream Whip
1 cup coconut

In a large mixing bowl, blend the cake mix and pudding mix with the oil, **Mello Yello®**, and flavorings for 2 minutes at medium speed. Add the eggs one at a time, beating well after each addition. Beat for 2 more minutes. Fold in the Dream Whip and coconut. Pour into a large greased and floured tube pan. Cook at 325 degrees for 1 hour and 10 minutes or until done.

Icing:

1 pound confectioners' sugar
1 stick butter
1/4 cup milk
1/2 teaspoon coconut flavoring
1 teaspoon lemon flavoring
1/2 cup coconut
2 drops yellow food coloring

Put the sugar in a bowl and make a well. Pour the melted butter into the well and mix together until it forms a ball. Add the milk until it reaches a spreadable consistency. Then add the flavorings, coconut and coloring.

Spread the icing over the cake while it is still warm. Let the icing run down the sides while spreading with a knife.

Poppy Seed Loaf Cake

3 cups flour, unsifted
1 1/2 teaspoons salt
1 1/2 teaspoons baking powder
3 eggs
1 1/8 cups oil
2 1/4 cups sugar
1 1/2 cups **Sprite®**
1/2 cup powdered milk
1 1/2 teaspoons almond flavoring
1 1/2 tablespoons poppy seeds
1 1/2 teaspoons vanilla
1 1/2 teaspoons butter flavoring

In a large mixing bowl, combine all of the ingredients and mix well for 2 minutes. Pour into 2 wax paper lined loaf pans. Bake 1 hour at 350 degrees.

Glaze:

1-1/4 cups **Minute Maid®** orange juice
3/4 cup sugar
1/2 teaspoon almond flavoring
1/2 teaspoon butter flavoring
1/2 teaspoon vanilla

Combine all of the ingredients and pour over the hot cake.

Apricot Nectar Cake

1 box lemon cake mix
1 package lemon Jell-O
3/4 cup apricot nectar
1/2 cup oil
1/2 teaspoon salt
1 teaspoon vanilla
4 eggs

In a large mixing bowl, combine the cake mix, Jell-O, nectar, oil salt and vanilla and mix well. Add the eggs, one at a time, beating well after each addition. Bake in a well greased and floured tube pan at 325 degrees for 50 minutes. While the cake is still hot, punch holes with a toothpick and pour the glaze over it. Let it stand overnight to absorb the flavor.

Glaze: Mix together

> 3 cups powdered sugar
> 1/4 cup lemon juice
> 3/4 cup **Minute Maid®** orange juice
> 2 tablespoons dried lemon peel

Peanut Butter Cake

> 1 box yellow cake mix
> 1 package French vanilla instant pudding mix
> 1/2 teaspoon nutmeg
> 1/2 cup oil
> 1 teaspoon butter flavoring
> 2 teaspoons vanilla butter and nut flavoring
> 1 cup **Sprite®**
> 4 eggs
> 3/4 cup nuts, chopped
> 1/2 cup peanut butter chips
> drizzle (see below)

In a large mixing bowl, combine the cake mix, pudding mix, nutmeg, oil, flavorings and **Sprite®** until well blended. Add the eggs one at a time, beating well after each addition. Fold in the nuts and peanut butter chips. Pour into a large greased and floured bundt pan. Bake at 350 degrees for 45 to 55 minutes or until done. Turn out with the top side up, drizzle cake while it is slightly warm.

Drizzle:

> 4 ounces peanut butter chips
> 1 tablespoon butter
> 1/4 cup **Sprite®**
> 1 cup confectioners' sugar
> 1 teaspoon vanilla
> dash of salt

In a saucepan, over low heat, melt the chips and butter in **Sprite®**. Add the sugar, vanilla and salt and beat until smooth.

Coconut Lemonade Loaf

1/4 cup finely ground coconut cookie crumbs
5 1/2 tablespoons butter or margarine, melted
1 cup sugar
2 eggs
1 1/2 cups all-purpose flour
1 teaspoon baking powder
1/4 teaspoon salt
1/2 cup milk
1 tablespoon **Minute Maid®** lemonade concentrate
1/2 cup finely chopped pecans

Lemonade Glaze

1/2 cup **Minute Maid®** lemonade concentrate
1/2 cup sugar
1/4 teaspoon coconut flavoring

Preheat the oven to 350 degrees. Generously grease a 9x5x3-inch loaf pan. Coat the pan with the cookie crumbs, shaking out any excess crumbs. In a large bowl, beat together the butter, sugar, and eggs. In a medium bowl, combine the flour, baking powder, and salt and stir to mix. Add to the egg mixture alternately with the milk, starting and ending with the flour mixture. Add the lemonade concentrate and mix well. Stir in the pecans. Pour the batter into the prepared loaf pan. Bake for 40 to 45 minutes, or until a wooden pick comes out clean when inserted into the center of the loaf.

While the loaf is baking, make the glaze. In a small saucepan, combine the lemonade concentrate with the sugar. Cook over medium heat until the sugar dissolves. Add coconut flavoring. Remove from heat.

As soon as the cake comes out of the oven, slowly spoon the lemonade glaze over the cake allowing it to seep into the cake. Cool in the pan. Remove from the pan and, when the loaf is completely cooled, wrap it securely with plastic wrap. It is best not to cut the cake for about 24 hours because it gets better the longer you wait. Securely wrapped, it will keep for a week.

Note: For serving as a finger sweet at a cocktail buffet, make miniature lemonade loaves using three (approximately 4-1/2x2x2-inch) pans. Bake for about 30 minutes. Cut the loaves into thin slices.

Russian Tea Cake

12 tablespoons butter or margarine, softened
1 1/4 cups sugar
1 teaspoon vanilla extract
3 eggs
2 cups all-purpose flour
1 tablespoon baking powder
1/2 teaspoon salt
1/3 cup instant tea mix with sugar and lemon
1 teaspoon ground cinnamon
1/4 teaspoon grated nutmeg
1/4 teaspoon ground cloves
1 cup **Minute Maid®** orange juice

Easy Caramel Icing:

1/4 pound butter or margarine, softened
1/4 cup firmly packed dark brown sugar
1/3 cup milk
1 teaspoon vanilla extract
1 (16 ounces) box confectioners' sugar

Preheat the oven to 350 degrees. Grease and lightly flour the bottom of a 9x13x2-inch baking pan. In a large mixing bowl, combine the butter, sugar, and vanilla extract. Beat until well blended. Add the eggs one at a time, beating well after each addition. In a medium bowl, combine the flour, baking powder, salt, tea mix, cinnamon, nutmeg, and cloves and stir to mix. Add to the batter alternately with the orange juice, starting and ending with the flour mixture. Pour into the prepared pan. Bake for about 25 minutes, or until a wooden pick inserted in the center of the cake comes out clean.

While the cake bakes, prepare the icing. In a medium saucepan, combine the butter, brown sugar, and milk and bring to a boil. Remove from the heat and stir in the vanilla extract and confectioners' sugar. Beat until smooth.

Pour the caramel icing over the top of the cake while it is still warm. Allow to cool completely on a rack before slicing.

Pound o' Orange Cake

1 box pound cake mix
1 small package vanilla instant pudding
1/2 cup salad oil
4 eggs
1/2 cup **Minute Maid®** orange juice
1/2 cup **Sprite®**

In a large mixing bowl, combine all of the ingredients and mix for 5 minutes on medium speed.

Pour into a greased and floured cake pan (bundt or pound). Bake at 325 degrees for 45 minutes to 1 hour.

Icing:

1 cup confectioners' sugar, sifted
1 tablespoon **Minute Maid®** orange juice
1 teaspoon vanilla

Mix all ingredients together and drizzle over cake while it is warm.

Chocolate Cherry Cake

1 box Swiss chocolate cake mix
1 box instant chocolate pudding
1 cup sour cream
1/2 teaspoon cherry extract
1/2 cup **cherry Coke®**
1/2 cup plus 1 tablespoon oil
5 eggs
1/2 cup maraschino cherries, sliced
3/4 cup dates, chopped
1/2 cup pecans, chopped
1 tablespoon flour

Preheat the oven to 325 degrees. In a large mixing bowl, blend the cake mix and pudding with the sour cream, flavoring, **cherry Coke®**, and oil for 2 minutes at medium speed.

Add the eggs one at a time, beating well after each addition. Stir in the cherries. Coat the dates and pecans with flour and fold into the batter.

Pour into a large bundt pan and bake at 325 degrees for 55 to 60 minutes or until done.

Chocolate Fudge Sheet Cake

1 cup **Coca-Cola®**
1/2 cup oil
1 stick margarine
3 tablespoons cocoa
2 cups sugar
2 cups flour
1/2 teaspoon salt
2 eggs
1/2 cup buttermilk
1 teaspoon baking soda
1 teaspoon vanilla

Icing:

1 stick butter or margarine
3 tablespoons cocoa
6 tablespoons cream or milk
1 teaspoon vanilla
1/2 to 1 cup pecans, chopped
1 pound confectioners' sugar

In a saucepan, bring the **Coca-Cola®**, oil, margarine and cocoa to a boil. In a bowl, mix the sugar, flour and salt. Pour in the boiling liquid

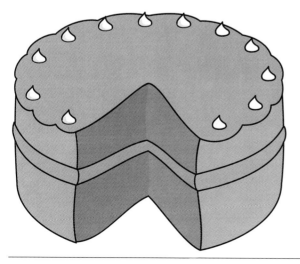

and beat well. Add the eggs, buttermilk, soda and vanilla and beat well. Pour into a greased and floured sheet cake pan and bake at 350 degrees for 20 to 25 minutes.

In a saucepan, combine the butter, cocoa, and milk and heat until the butter melts. Beat in the remaining ingredients. Spread on the hot cake. Cool and cut.

Chocolate Chip Cake

1 box yellow cake mix
1 box instant vanilla pudding
4 eggs
1 cup **Sprite®**
1/3 cup powdered milk
1 cup cooking oil
4 ounce bar cooking chocolate, grated
6 ounces chocolate chips
1/4 cup confectioners sugar

In a large mixing bowl, combine the cake mix, pudding, eggs, **Sprite®**, powdered milk and oil. Beat for 2 minutes. Stir in the grated chocolate and chocolate chips. Pour into a well-oiled and floured bundt or tube pan. (Cocoa may be used instead of flour.) Bake at 350 degrees for about 1 hour. Test for doneness and cook longer, if necessary. Sprinkle with confectioners' sugar.

PIE

Own Crust Pie

4 eggs
1/2 stick butter
2 cups **Sprite®**
2/3 cup powdered milk
1 cup shredded coconut
1/2 teaspoon baking powder
1 cup sugar
1/2 cup flour
1/4 teaspoon salt
1 teaspoon vanilla

Combine all the ingredients in a blender and mix until smooth. Pour into a well greased 10 inch pie pan. Bake at 350 degrees for 1 hour and 5 minutes. Crust will form on bottom, custard in middle and coconut on top.

Blender Pie

2 cups **Sprite®**
2/3 cup powdered milk
1 1/2 teaspoons vanilla
1/2 cup Bisquick mix
1/2 stick butter
3/4 cup sugar
1 cup coconut
4 eggs

Place all the ingredients in the blender and blend for 3 minutes. Pour into pie pan and allow to set for 5 minutes.

Bake at 350 degrees for 40 minutes. Makes its own crust.

Quick and Easy Lime Pie

8 ounce carton whipped topping
1 can sweetened condensed milk
1 can (6 ounces) **Minute Maid®** limeade concentrate
green food coloring (optional)
1 pie shell (pastry or graham cracker)

Mix the whipped topping and condensed milk; stir in the limeade concentrate. Add 2 to 3 drops of food coloring, if desired.

Mix thoroughly and pour into the pie shell. Chill for a couple of hours.

Lemonade Pie

1 can (6 ounces) **Minute Maid®** lemonade concentrate
8 ounces Cool Whip
1 can sweetened condensed milk
graham cracker pie crust

Mix the lemonade concentrate, Cool Whip, and milk together until well blended. Pour into the pie crust and refrigerate until firm.

Garnish the top of pie with slices of lemon or lime, or sprinkle graham cracker crumbs on top.

Lemon-Lime Pie

1 cup sugar, divided
1 envelope (1 tablespoon) unflavored gelatin
1/8 teaspoon salt
1 cup **Coca-Cola®**
3 eggs, separated
1/4 cup fresh lemon juice
1/4 cup fresh lime juice
1 cup whipped topping or whipped cream
1 9-inch graham cracker or chocolate cookie crust
    or baked pie shell
2 tablespoons grated lime peel

In the top of a double boiler, stir together the gelatin, 1/2 cup of the sugar, and salt. Stir in the **Coca-Cola®**. Beat the egg yolks and add to the **Coca-Cola®** mixture. Cook over boiling water, stirring constantly until the gelatin is dissolved, about 5 minutes. Remove from the heat and stir in the lemon and lime juice. Chill until the mixture mounds when dropped from a spoon. Beat the egg whites until soft peaks form. Gradually beat in the remaining 1/2 cup sugar, beating until stiff and glossy. Fold the gelatin mixture into the whipped topping then carefully fold this into egg whites. Chill for several minutes then pile into the pie crust and sprinkle with the grated lime peel. Chill for several hours until firm. If desired, top with a dollop of whipped cream.

Chocolate Surprise

1 cup flour
1 stick butter or margarine, melted
1/2 cup nuts, chopped
8 ounces cream cheese, softened
1 cup powdered sugar
1 cup Cool Whip
2 packages (4 ounces each) instant fudge pudding
3 cups **Coca-Cola®**
1 cup powdered milk

Combine the flour, butter, and nuts and press into a 9x13 greased pyrex dish. Bake at 350 degrees for 20 minutes. Cool. Mix the cream cheese, powdered sugar, and Cool Whip. Spread over the first layer and chill. Mix the pudding, powdered milk, and **Coca-Cola®**. Beat with a wire whisk until thick. Spread on top of the cream cheese layer and chill. When ready to serve, cut into squares, top with whipped cream and cherry.

Instant Chocolate Pie

8 inch graham cracker pie crust
4 1/2 ounce package instant chocolate pudding mix
1/3 cup powdered milk
1 cup **Fresca®**
2 cups non-dairy whipped topping
1/4 cup chopped pecans
chopped pecans

Bake the pie shell and let cool. Combine the pudding mix, powdered milk and **Fresca®** and let set for 5 minutes. Blend in 1 1/2 cups of the whipped topping and 1/4 cup pecans. Spoon into the pie shell and decorate with the remaining 1/2 cup whipped topping and additional nuts. Chill for at least 1 hour.

Variation: Use banana pudding mix instead of chocolate and 2 bananas instead of pecans.

Easy Cobbler

1 1/2 sticks margarine
2 cups sugar
1 1/2 cups flour
1 1/2 cups **Sprite®**
1/2 cup powdered milk
4 cups fruit (fresh or canned)
4 teaspoons baking powder
1 teaspoon salt

In a 9x13 inch glass baking dish, melt the margarine. In a bowl, mix the flour, sugar, baking powder, salt and powdered milk. Stir in the **Sprite®**. Pour the batter into the casserole dish. DO NOT STIR.

Spoon the fruit over the batter. DO NOT STIR. Bake at 350 degrees for 30 minutes.

Strawberry Pie

3/4 cup flour
6 tablespoons margarine
1/3 cup nuts, chopped fine
3 tablespoons brown sugar
1 cup strawberries, sliced
1 cup whipping cream
1 tablespoon sugar
1 cup **Fresca®**
1/3 cup powdered milk
1 package instant vanilla pudding mix

Preheat the oven to 425 degrees. In a bowl, combine the flour, margarine, nuts, and brown sugar. Mix by hand until crumbly. Press the mixture into a 9-inch pie pan. Place an 8-inch cake pan on top and bake for 15 minutes. Remove the cake pan and let cool. Whip the cream and sugar until soft peaks form and set aside. Mix the pudding mix and powdered milk in a bowl, add the **Fresca®** and beat well for 2 minutes. Immediately fold the whipped cream and strawberries into the pudding and pour into the shell. Chill until firm.

Raisin Crisscross Pie

1 cup packed brown sugar
3 tablespoons cornstarch
2 cups raisins
1 1/3 cups **Sprite®**
1 teaspoon finely shredded orange peel
1/2 cup **Minute Maid®** Orange Juice
1 teaspoon finely shredded lemon peel
2 tablespoons lemon juice
1/2 cup broken walnuts
pastry for a lattice top pie

In a medium saucepan, combine the brown sugar and cornstarch. Stir in the raisins, **Sprite®**, orange peel, orange juice, lemon peel, and lemon juice. Cook, stirring constantly, until the mixture is thickened and bubbly. Continue cooking and stirring for 1 minute more. Remove from the heat and stir in the nuts. Fill the pie crust with the raisin mixture and adjust the lattice top. Seal and flute the edges. Bake in 350 degree oven for about 30 minutes.

Cranberry Raisin Pie

3 cups cranberries
1 cup light raisins
1 cup **Sprite®**
1/4 cup lemon juice
3/4 cup packed brown sugar
2 tablespoons cornstarch
1/2 teaspoon salt
1/2 teaspoon ground cinnamon
1/2 teaspoon ground nutmeg
3/4 cup grape jam
pastry for a lattice top pie

In a medium saucepan combine the cranberries, raisins, **Sprite®**, and lemon juice; cook and stir for about 8 minutes or until the cranberries have popped. Combine the brown sugar, cornstarch, salt, cinnamon and nutmeg and add to the hot cranberry mixture. Cook quickly, stirring constantly, until thickened and bubbly. Remove from the heat and stir in the grape jam until melted. Fill the pie crust with the cranberry mixture and adjust the lattice top. Seal and flute the edges and cover the edges with foil.

Bake in 375 degree oven for 20 minutes; remove the foil and bake 15 to 20 minutes longer. Cool before serving.

Fresh Fruit Pie

1/2 cup sugar
3 tablespoons cornstarch
1 1/2 cups **Minute Maid®** orange juice
1/4 cup lemon juice
1 teaspoon grated lemon rind
6 cups assorted fresh fruit, drained, cut in bite size pieces
graham cracker crust

In a saucepan, mix the sugar and cornstarch. Gradually add the orange juice until smooth. Bring to a boil over medium heat, stirring constantly, and boil for 1 minute. Remove from the heat and stir in the lemon juice and grated rind. Cool completely. Fold in the fresh fruit. Turn into pie crust. Chill 4 hours.

Sprite® Apple Pie

Butterscotch Crust:

1/2 cup butterscotch morsels
1 1/4 cups all-purpose flour
1/8 teaspoon salt
3/4 cup chopped walnuts
1/4 pound butter or margarine, softened

Filling:

3/4 cup **Sprite®**
1/3 cup sugar
2 teaspoons lemon juice
3 1/2 cups peeled and chopped Granny Smith apples
8 ounces cream cheese, softened
2 cups confectioners' sugar
1/2 cup heavy cream, whipped

Preheat the oven to 350 degrees. Combine the butterscotch morsels, flour, salt and walnuts in the bowl of a food processor fitted with the steel blade. Process until the mixture is almost as fine as flour. Add the butter and process until mixed.

Press the mixture into a 9-inch pie plate. Bake for about 15 minutes, until lightly browned. If the shell puffed up while cooking, quickly flatten it with your fingertips before it cools. Cool completely before adding the filling.

Combine the **Sprite®**, sugar, lemon juice, and chopped apples in a medium pan. Cook over medium-high heat about 3 to 4 minutes, or until tender but not mushy. Remove from the heat. Drain and cool completely. In a large mixing bowl, combine the cream cheese and confectioners' sugar and beat until smooth. Stir in the whipped cream, add the cooled apple mixture, and spoon into pie crust. Refrigerate.

Banana-Apricot Pie

2 cups dried apricots, snipped
1 1/2 cups **Sprite®**
1 1/4 cups sugar

1/4 cup all purpose flour
1/4 teaspoon salt
3 egg yolks, slightly beaten
2 tablespoons butter or margarine
2 medium bananas, thinly sliced
baked pie shell
meringue

In a saucepan, combine the apricots and **Sprite®**. Cover and simmer for 10 minutes or until tender. In a bowl, combine the sugar, flour, and salt and stir into the apricot mixture.

Cook, stirring constantly, until the mixture is thickened and bubbly. Continue cooking and stirring for 2 minutes more.

Stir 1 cup of the hot mixture into the egg yolks and return it to the saucepan. Return the mixture to a gentle boil. Cook and stir for 2 minutes.

Stir in the butter. Arrange the bananas in the pie shell and pour the apricot mixture on top. Spread meringue over the hot filling. Bake in 350 degree oven for 12 to 15 minutes.

Serve warm or cool.

COOKIES

Lemonade Cookies

3 cups sifted flour
1 teaspoon baking soda
1 cup butter or margarine, softened
1 cup sugar
1 can (6 ounces) **Minute Maid®** lemonade concentrate

Sift together the flour and baking soda. Add the butter, sugar and lemonade concentrate. Drop by teaspoons onto a cookie sheet.

Bake for 8 minutes at 400 degrees.

Option: When done, brush with lemonade and sprinkle with sugar.

Fruitcake Cookies

1 box white raisins
1/2 pound red cherries
1/4 pound green cherries
1/4 pound pineapple, chopped
6 cups chopped nuts
1 1/2 cups brown sugar
4 eggs beaten
1 cup **Coca-Cola®**
3 1/2 cups self-rising flour
1 stick margarine, softened

Place all of fruit in a bowl and mix 1/2 cup of the flour with it, then add the nuts. In a separate bowl, mix the remaining ingredients well. Add to fruit mixture and mix by hand. Drop by teaspoons on a cookie sheet. Bake at 300 degrees for 15 to 18 minutes or until light brown.

Makes a large quantity and freezes well.

Boiled Oatmeal Raisin Cookies

2 cups **Coca-Cola®**
15 ounce package raisins
1 1/4 cups cooking oil
1 3/4 cups sugar
3 eggs, beaten
4 cups flour, sifted
2 teaspoons baking powder
1 teaspoon salt
4 cups oatmeal
2 cups nuts
2 teaspoons baking soda
1 teaspoon cinnamon
1 teaspoon nutmeg
1 teaspoon cloves
1 teaspoon ginger
6 ounces chocolate chips (optional)

Boil the raisins in **Coca-Cola®**, covered, for 20 minutes. Add the oil and sugar. Cool and add the remaining ingredients. Drop by teaspoons onto cookie sheet. Bake at 350 degrees for 12 to 15 minutes.

PUDDINGS

Dirt Dessert

16 ounce package Oreo cookies
12 ounces Cool Whip
8 ounces cream cheese, softened
1 cup powdered sugar
1 stick margarine, softened
2 cups **Fresca®**
2/3 cup powdered milk
1 box (3 ounce) French vanilla instant pudding mix
1 teaspoon vanilla

Crush the Oreos and place half the crumbs in the bottom of an 11x17 inch pan. Use a mixer to blend the Cool Whip, cream cheese, powdered sugar, and margarine. In a bowl, combine the pudding mix, powdered milk, **Fresca®**, and vanilla.

Beat this mixture until it is the consistency of pudding. Combine both mixtures and pour over the layer of crushed Oreos.

Sprinkle the remaining Oreos on top. Refrigerate for 1 to 2 hours before serving.

Oreo Dirt Cups

2 cups **Fresca®**
2/3 cup powdered milk
1 large package instant chocolate pudding mix
8 ounces Cool Whip
16 ounce package Oreo cookies, crushed fine

In a large bowl, mix the powdered milk, chocolate pudding mix, and **Fresca®**. Beat until well-blended. Let set for 5 minutes. Stir in the Cool Whip and half the crushed Oreos. Place 1 tablespoon of crushed Oreos into the bottom of each of 8 dessert cups. Fill each cup 3/4 full with the pudding mixture.

Top with the remaining cookies. Chill for at least 1 hour.

Chocolate Delight

1 cup flour
1 stick margarine, softened
1/4 cup sugar
1/2 cup chopped nuts
8 ounces cream cheese, softened
1 cup powdered sugar
1 cup Cool Whip
2 small packages instant chocolate pudding
3 cups **Fresca®**
1 cup powdered milk
1 cup Cool Whip
chopped nuts or shredded chocolate

In a bowl, combine the flour, margarine, 1/4 cup sugar, and 1/2 cup chopped nuts. Press into a 9x13 inch pan and bake for 15 to 20 minutes at 375 degrees. Let cool. Mix the cream cheese and powdered sugar together. Add 1 cup Cool Whip and spread on top of the baked layer. Mix the chocolate pudding, powdered milk and **Fresca®**. Let set for five minutes. Spread on top of the cream cheese layer. Top with Cool Whip. Sprinkle with nuts or shredded chocolate.

Blueberry Delight

14 whole graham crackers, plain or cinnamon
1 package instant vanilla pudding mix
8 ounces **Fresca®**
1/3 cup powdered milk
1 cup Cool Whip, thawed
1 can (21 ounces) blueberry pie filling

Place a layer of graham crackers in the bottom of a 9 inch square pan (8 inch will not do). Combine the pudding mix, **Fresca®**, and milk and let stand for 5 minutes. Blend in the Cool Whip. Spread half of the pudding mix over the graham crackers. Add another layer of graham crackers. Top with remaining pudding mix and remaining graham crackers. Spread the pie filling over the top layer of graham crackers. Chill for 3 hours.

Note: For Cherry Delight, substitute cherry pie filling.

Coca-Cola® Sparkler

1 package lemon gelatin
1/2 cup boiling water
12 ounces **Coca-Cola®**
whipped cream

Pour the boiling water over the gelatin and stir until the gelatin dissolves. Let cool and add the **Coca-Cola®**. Chill until firm. Serve topped with whipped cream.

Coca-Cola® Fluff

1 package lime gelatin
12 ounces **Coca-Cola®**
2/3 cup boiling water
1 cup heavy cream, whipped

Pour the boiling water over the gelatin and stir until the gelatin is dissolved. Let cool slightly. Add the **Coca-Cola®** and mix thoroughly. Cool and refrigerate. When the gelatin begins to congeal, beat with a mixer until frothy. Fold in the whipped cream and chill.

Baked Pineapple Tapioca

1 can (20 ounce) pineapple chunks, juice pack
3/4 cup **Sprite®**
1/2 cup sugar
3 tablespoons quick-cooking tapioca
1 tablespoon lemon juice
1/2 teaspoon salt
dash ground nutmeg
whipped dessert topping
1/2 cup chopped walnuts

In a bowl combine the undrained pineapple, **Sprite®**, sugar, tapioca, lemon juice, salt, and nutmeg. Let the mixture stand for 10 minutes. Pour the mixture into a 1-quart casserole dish. Bake, uncovered, in 325 degree oven 40 to 50 minutes or until the tapioca granules are clear and the pudding is thick; stir occasionally. Cool slightly and serve topped with whipped dessert topping and sprinkled with chopped walnuts.

Lemonade Fluff Parfaits

1/2 cup sugar
3 tablespoons cornstarch
1/4 teaspoon salt
1 1/2 cups milk
2 egg yolks, beaten
1 package (3 ounces) cream cheese, softened
2 tablespoons butter or margarine
1 teaspoon vanilla
1/2 cup **Minute Maid®** lemonade concentrate
2 egg whites
1/4 cup sugar
1/2 cup crushed vanilla wafers (12 cookies)
2 tablespoons chopped walnuts
2 tablespoons butter or margarine, melted

In a saucepan combine the 1/2 cup sugar, cornstarch, and salt; stir in the milk. Cook over medium heat, stirring constantly, until thickened and bubbly. Remove from heat. Gradually add 1 cup of the hot mixture to the beaten egg yolks, mixing well. Return the mixture to the saucepan; cook and stir for 2 minutes more.

Remove from heat. Add the cream cheese, 2 tablespoons butter and vanilla; beat with a rotary beater until smooth.

Stir in the lemonade concentrate. Cover the surface with waxed paper to prevent a skin from forming. Cool for 10 minutes. With clean beaters, beat the egg whites to soft peaks; gradually add the 1/4 cup sugar and beat to stiff peaks. Fold into the pudding mixture.

In a bowl, combine the cookie crumbs, nuts and melted butter. Layer the pudding and crumbs in parfait glasses, beginning with pudding and ending with crumbs. Cover and chill.

Strawberry Trifle

1/4 cup granulated sugar
2 tablespoons cornstarch
16 ounce package frozen strawberries, thawed
1 tablespoon lemon juice

2 eggs
1 egg yolk
1 3/4 cups milk
1/4 cup granulated sugar
8 cups cubed sponge cake
3/4 cup **Sprite®**
1 egg white
1 tablespoon sifted powdered sugar
1 cup whipping cream
1/4 teaspoon vanilla
1/4 cup slivered almonds

In a saucepan, stir together 1/4 cup granulated sugar and cornstarch. Add the strawberries with their syrup.

Cook and stir over medium heat about 10 minutes or until thick and bubbly. Stir in the lemon juice. Cover the surface of the mixture with waxed paper to prevent a skin from forming and cool.

In a heavy saucepan combine the eggs, egg yolk, milk, and 1/4 cup granulated sugar. Cook and stir about 10 minutes or until the custard coats a metal spoon; remove from heat.

Pour the custard into a medium-size bowl and place it inside a larger bowl filled with ice. Stir for 1 to 2 minutes to hasten cooling.

Place 3 cups of cake cubes into a 2-quart serving dish. Sprinkle with 1/4 cup **Sprite®**. Reserve 1/4 cup of the strawberry mixture for garnish. Top cake cubes with half the remaining strawberry mixture and half of the custard. Repeat layers using another 3 cups of cake cubes, 1/4 cup **Sprite®**, the remaining strawberry mixture and the remaining custard.

Add the remaining cake cubes and sprinkle with the remaining **Sprite®**. Beat the egg white to soft peaks.

Add the powdered sugar and beat until stiff peaks form. Whip the cream and vanilla together to soft peaks; fold into the egg white. Spread the mixture on top of the cake cubes.

Refrigerate for 6 hours or overnight. Just before serving, dot with the reserved strawberry mixture and sprinkle with almonds.

Chocolate Rice Pudding

1 1/2 cups **Sprite®**
1/2 cup powdered milk
1/2 cup long grain rice
1/2 cup raisins
2 squares semi-sweet chocolate (1 ounce each)
2 tablespoons butter or margarine
2 tablespoons sugar
1 tablespoon cornstarch
1/2 cup **Coca-Cola®**
2 beaten egg yolks
2 egg whites
1/4 cup sugar

In a saucepan combine the **Sprite®**, powdered milk, rice and raisins. Simmer, covered, for 25 to 30 minutes or until rice is tender. In a medium saucepan over low heat, melt the chocolate and butter. Combine the 2 tablespoons of sugar and cornstarch. Stir into the chocolate; add the **Coca-Cola®** and egg yolks. Cook and stir until bubbly. Stir in the rice mixture. In a mixing bowl, beat the egg whites to soft peaks. Gradually add the 1/4 cup sugar and beat to stiff peaks. Fold into the rice mixture. Cover and chill.

Honey Rice Pudding

2 cups water
2 cups **Sprite®**
1 1/3 cups powdered milk
1/2 cup long grain rice
1/2 cup raisins (optional)
1/4 cup honey
1/2 teaspoon salt
1/2 teaspoon vanilla
1/2 teaspoon ground cinnamon

In a 1 1/2 quart casserole dish, combine all of the ingredients except the cinnamon. Bake, uncovered, at 300 degrees about 2 hours, stirring gently every 20 minutes.

Sprinkle with the cinnamon. Serve warm.

Holiday Bread Pudding

2 slightly beaten eggs
2 1/4 cups **Sprite®**
3/4 cup powdered milk
1/2 cup packed brown sugar
1 teaspoon vanilla
1/4 teaspoon salt
5 slices day-old white bread, cut into 1 inch pieces
1/3 cup raisins

In a mixing bowl combine the eggs, **Sprite®**, milk, brown sugar, vanilla, and salt; stir in the bread pieces and raisins. Let stand 5 minutes. Turn the mixture into an ungreased 8 x 1 1/2 inch round baking dish. Place the dish in a 13x9x2 inch baking pan. Carefully pour hot water into the larger pan to a depth of 1 inch. Bake uncovered, in 350 degree oven about 50 minutes or until a knife inserted in the center comes out clean. Serve warm.

Chocolate Bread Pudding

4 beaten eggs
2 2/3 cups **Sprite®**
1 cup powdered milk
1/2 cup sugar
1-1/2 teaspoons vanilla
1 teaspoon ground cinnamon
1/2 teaspoon salt
4 cups dry bread cubes (6 slices)
3/4 cup tiny semisweet chocolate pieces
1/3 cup chopped walnuts

In a mixing bowl, combine the eggs, **Sprite®**, milk, sugar, vanilla, cinnamon and salt. Stir in the bread cubes, chocolate, and nuts. Turn the mixture into an ungreased 10x6x2 inch baking dish. Place the dish in a 13x9x2 inch baking pan. Carefully pour hot water into the larger pan to a depth of 1 inch.

Bake in 350 degree oven for 65 to 70 minutes or until a knife inserted just off-center comes out clean. Serve warm.

Toffee Pistachio Delight

1 small package instant pistachio pudding
1 cup **Fresca®**
1/3 cup powdered milk
6 ounces vanilla wafers, crushed
7 ounces frozen whipped topping, thawed
7 ounces Heath candy bars, finely chopped

Mix the pudding, powdered milk and **Fresca®** and let set for 5 minutes. In a 9x9 inch pan, layer half the crushed wafers, half the pudding, half the whipped topping and half the chopped candy bars. Repeat the layers, ending with the candy bars for garnish. Refrigerate overnight.

ICE CREAM

Orange-Chocolate Pops

1 pint chocolate ice cream
1 cup chocolate milk
3 oz (1/2 can) **Minute Maid®** orange juice concentrate
1/4 cup powdered sugar
10 wooden sticks

In a blender container, combine the ice cream, milk, orange juice concentrate and sugar. Cover and blend until smooth. Pour into ten 3-ounce waxed paper drink cups.

Freeze until they reach a thick slushy consistency. Insert wooden sticks and freeze firm.

To serve, peel off the paper cup wrapping.

Deluxe Fruit Ice Cream

2 ripe medium bananas, cut up
2 cups chopped pitted fresh apricots
1 pint fresh strawberries
1 cup **Minute Maid®** orange juice

1/2 cup lemon juice
3 cups milk
2 cups sugar
2 cups whipping cream
1/4 teaspoon salt

Place the bananas, apricots, strawberries, orange juice, and lemon juice in a blender container; cover and blend at medium speed until smooth. Turn the mixture out into a large bowl.

In the same blender container, combine the milk, sugar, whipping cream and salt; cover and blend until smooth.

Stir the milk mixture into the fruit mixture. Freeze in a 4- or 5-quart ice cream freezer.

Cherry Coke® Ice Cream

2 cups **cherry Coke®**
dash salt
2 cans evaporated milk
2 cups sugar
1 pint whipping cream
1 jar cherries, chopped
milk, if needed to fill freezer

Mix all the ingredients together, except the milk, and pour into a 4- or 5-quart ice cream freezer. Add milk to reach the "fill line." Freeze according to the freezer directions.

Floating Frog

Lime sherbert
Sprite®
Raisins
Large marshmallows

Place 1 scoop of sherbert into a clear dessert dish. Put 1 marshmallow on top of the sherbert. Put 2 raisins on the marshmallow for eyes. Cover the sherbert and marshmallow completely with **Sprite®**.

Wait and watch the frog float.

From a 1946 advertising campaign. (Courtesy of The Coca-Cola Company.)

CHAPTER 12

CANDIES

W e only have a few candy recipes, but they are *fine* ones. The Walnut Balls below are especially rich and delightful. If you are going to eat candy, *this* is the type to eat. There's no need to settle for less than the best. Enjoy!

Walnut Balls

1 cup chopped walnuts
1/4 cup **Coca-Cola®**
1 box powdered sugar
1/2 cup butter or margarine, melted
1 package (8 ounces)
      unsweetened chocolate
1 tablespoon shortening

Soak the nuts in **Coca-Cola®** for at least 3 hours. Combine the nuts, sugar and butter. Shape into 3/4 inch balls and chill for at least 30 minutes. Combine the chocolate and shortening in the top of a double boiler. Heat until melted and smooth, stirring occasionally. Using a wooden pick, dip each ball into the chocolate and place on a waxed paper-lined baking sheet to dry. Chill until they are firm and store the balls in the refrigerator.

Orange Balls

12 ounces vanilla wafer crumbs
16 ounces powdered sugar
1/2 cup butter, softened
6 ounces **Minute Maid®** orange juice concentrate
1 cup nuts, finely chopped
flaked coconut (optional)

Combine the cookie crumbs, powdered sugar, butter, juice concentrate and nuts. Mix well with hands and form into bite-size balls. If desired, roll in flaked coconut. Chill until firm. Makes about 60 balls.

May be stored in the refrigerator for up to 2 weeks and they are ready to serve at room temperature in minutes.

Orange Candy

1 1/2 cups sugar
3 cups English walnuts
1/2 cup **Minute Maid®** orange juice concentrate
2 teaspoons orange extract
dash of salt
1 teaspoon corn syrup
4 drops red food coloring
3 drops yellow food coloring

In a saucepan, combine all ingredients except food coloring and walnuts. Cook over medium heat until the mixture reaches soft ball stage. Remove from heat and stir in the food coloring. Add the walnuts and stir until creamy. Pour onto wax paper. Use forks to separate into bite size pieces.

Georgia Goober Creams

1 cup chopped peanuts
3/4 cup **Coca-Cola®**
2 cups light brown sugar, firmly packed
pinch of salt
3 tablespoons margarine

Mix brown sugar, **Coke®**, and salt in a saucepan. Stir over low heat until sugar dissolves. Cook to 236 degrees on candy therometer, or until a small amount of mixture dropped into cold water forms a soft ball. Remove from heat and cool to 110 degrees, or until candy is lukewarm. Place peanuts and butter in a baking pan. Bake in oven at 450 degrees for 8 to 10 minutes. Add peanuts and butter to mixture after it cools and beat until mixture is no longer glossy. Put into a lightly greased 9 x 9 x 3-inch pan and cool.

Cut into squares. Makes about 1 pound of candy.

Pecan Hurrah

1/2 pound pecan halves
1/2 cup **Coca-Cola®**
1 cup sugar
3/4 teaspoon cinnamon
1/4 teaspoon nutmeg
1 teaspoon salt

Put pecans on a baking sheet. Roast for 15 minutes in a 250-degree oven. Mix **Coca-Cola®**, sugar, salt, and spices in a saucepan. Cook to 236 degrees on candy thermometer (soft-ball stage). Do not stir. Stir in pecans until thoroughly coated and creamy.

Pour onto waxed paper and let cool slightly. Separate pecans, and let cool completely.

Walnut Candy

4 cups walnut halves
1/2 cup **Sprite®**
1 1/2 cups sugar
1/4 cup honey
1/2 teaspoon vanilla
grated rind of 1 orange

Mix **Sprite®**, honey, and sugar, and cook to soft-ball stage (236 degrees on a candy thermometer). Add the walnuts, vanilla, and orange rind. Stir carefully until syrup is thick and creamy.

Pour onto a sheet of wax paper, quickly separating the nuts. Let cool.

Atlanta Butterscotch Fudge

1 package butterscotch pudding
1/2 cup **Coca-Cola®**
1/4 cup powdered milk
1 1/2 cups chopped pecans
1/2 cup brown sugar, packed
1 cup sugar
1 tablespoon margarine or butter
1 teaspoon vanilla

Mix pudding, brown sugar, sugar, **Coca-Cola®**, and milk in a saucepan and bring to a boil. Cook for 5 minutes while stirring constantly. Remove from heat and add remaining ingredients.

Beat until cool.

Pour into a buttered dish and cut into squares.

Really good!

This ad for **Coca-Cola**® appeared in 1900 and featured actress Hilda Clarke. (Courtesy of The Archives of The Coca-Cola Company, Atlanta.)

CHAPTER 13

BEVERAGES

Yes, we know, **Coca-Cola®** is already a drink, but mixing other stuff in it is another of those long-standing traditions. Lemon, cherry, lime—all these flavors and more go well in **Coke®**. The Coca-Cola Company owns Minute Maid, and we include those products also. So we now present you with a whole raft of sweet, icy ways to cool off on a hot summer's day.

Banana Fruit Punch

3 1/2 cups sugar
6 cups water
3 cups pineapple juice
2 cups **Minute Maid®** orange juice
juice of 2 lemons
3 large or 4 small bananas, mashed
2 liter bottle **Sprite®**

Dissolve the sugar in the water. Add all of the other ingredients, except the **Sprite®**. Freeze for about 24 hours in a 6 quart container with a lid. About 2 to 3 hours before serving, remove it from the freezer and thaw to a slushy consistency. Mash out any lumps with a potato masher. Add **Sprite®** when ready to serve.

Orange Delightful

1 cup milk
1 cup **Sprite®**
1 can (6 ounces) **Minute Maid®** orange juice concentrate
1 teaspoon vanilla
1/4 cup sugar
10 ice cubes

Blend the milk, **Sprite®**, and orange juice in a blender on high for 3 seconds. Add the vanilla, sugar and ice cubes. Blend on high for 1 minute.

Fruity Ice Ring Punch

1 1/2 quarts water
2 orange slices, quartered
8 maraschino cherries
1 can (46 ounce) red fruit juice, chilled
2 1/2 cups pineapple juice, chilled
12 ounces Cherry **Coke®**, chilled

The day before serving, prepare the ice ring: Pour 1 cup of water into a 1 1/2 quart ring mold. Arrange the orange pieces and the maraschino cherries alternately in the bottom of the mold and freeze until firm. Fill the mold with water and freeze until solid. In a large punch bowl, combine the fruit juice and pineapple juice and mix well. Add the Cherry **Coke®**. Unmold and float the ice ring in the punch.

Georgia Punch

1 can (46 ounces) red fruit juice, chilled
1 1/2 cups **Minute Maid®** orange juice, chilled
1/4 cup fresh lemon juice
1 package (10 ounces) frozen sliced strawberries,
        partially thawed
2 12-ounce cans **Sprite®**, chilled
ice cubes

In a large punch bowl, combine the fruit juices and stir in the strawberries. Just before serving, add the **Sprite®** and ice. Garnish with lemon or lime slices, if desired.

Perky Punch

1 can (46 ounces) pineapple juice, chilled
1 can apricot nectar, chilled
1 can (6 ounces) **Minute Maid®** lemonade concentrate
4 cans (12 ounces each) **Sprite®**, chilled
ice cubes

In a large punch bowl, combine the pineapple juice, apricot nectar and lemonade concentrate and mix until well blended. Just before serving, add the **Sprite®** and ice.

Garnish with flowers or mint leaves, if desired.

Sunny Day Punch

1 can (46 ounces) red fruit juice, chilled
1 1/2 cups pineapple juice, chilled
1/4 cup lime juice
2 cans (12 ounces each) **Sprite®**, chilled
ice cubes

In a large punch bowl, combine the fruit juices and mix well. Just before serving, add the **Sprite®**. Serve over ice.

Party Punch

3 bananas, mashed
1 package unsweetened cherry Kool-Aid
1 package unsweetened orange Kool-Aid
1/2 cup lemon juice
1 can (46 ounces) unsweetened pineapple juice
1 1/2 quarts water
2 1/2 cups sugar
48 ounces **Sprite®**

Mix the bananas, Kool-Aid, juices, water and sugar well. Freeze in empty milk cartons. Thaw 4 to 6 hours before serving and add the **Sprite®**.

Banana Slush

6 cups water
3 1/2 cups sugar
2 cups **Minute Maid®** orange juice
3 cups pineapple juice
juice of 4 lemons
5 bananas
2 quarts **Sprite®**, chilled

Stir the sugar and water together until the sugar is dissolved. Mash the bananas and add the lemon juice. Stir the bananas into the sugar water. Add the orange and pineapple juices. Freeze this mixture. Slightly thaw the mixture before serving. Mash until it reaches a slushy consistency, then add **Sprite®**.

Strawberry Cooler

1 pint fresh strawberries, cleaned and sliced
1/3 to 1/2 cup sugar
1/4 cup **Minute Maid®** orange juice
1/2 cup pineapple juice
1 quart **Fresca®**
1 pint pineapple sherbert

Mash the strawberries and stir in the sugar. Add the juices and **Fresca®**. Pour into 4 chilled tall glasses. Top each glass with a scoop of sherbert. (Note: frozen strawberries may be substituted for fresh ones—use one 10-ounce package and omit the sugar.)

Strawberry-Lemonade Punch

1 can (6 ounces) **Minute Maid®** lemonade concentrate
1 can (6 ounces) **Minute Maid®** limeade concentrate
1 can (6 ounces) **Minute Maid®** orange juice concentrate
2 packages frozen sliced strawberries, thawed
3 cups cold water
2 liters **Fresca®**

Combine the first 5 ingredients and stir well. Add the **Fresca®** and stir gently.

Grape Cooler

1/2 cup sugar
2 cups water
1 cup grape juice
1 cup **Minute Maid®** orange juice
1/2 cup lemon juice
Sprite®

In a saucepan, combine the sugar and water. Cook over low heat until the mixture becomes clear. Let cool. Add the fruit juices. Pour over ice in tall glasses until half full, finish filling with **Sprite®**.

Mock Champagne

1 bottle **Sprite®**
1 bottle white grape juice

Chill the ingredients and mix well.

Cherry Coke® Punch

1/2 cup sugar
1 cup boiling water
1 cup ice water
1/2 cup lemon juice
1 cup pineapple juice
1 cup **Minute Maid®** orange juice
6 bottles (6 ounce size) **Coca-Cola®** (or 36 ounces **Coke®**)
1/2 cup minced maraschino cherries

Dissolve the sugar in the boiling water and add the ice water. When the mixture is cool, add the remaining ingredients. Serve in a punch bowl.

Coca-Cola® Triangle Punch

1 cup **Minute Maid®** orange juice
2 cups pineapple juice
6 bottles (6 ounce size) ice-cold **Coca-Cola®**

Combine the ingredients in the order given. Pour over ice in a punch bowl.

New Year's Coca-Cola® Punch

8 bottles (6 ounce size) ice-cold **Coca-Cola®**
1 cup **Minute Maid®** orange juice
1 cup pineapple juice
juice of 2 lemons

Combine the fruit juices and chill. Stir in the **Coca-Cola®** and serve
at once.

Fruit Punch

2 packages orange Jell-O
2 cups sugar
1 quart boiling water
1 quart cold water
12 ounces **Minute Maid®** lemonade concentrate
1 large can pineapple juice
12 ounces **Minute Maid®** orange juice concentrate
bottle **Fresca®**

Mix the Jell-O and sugar. Add the boiling water and stir to dissolve the
Jell-o and sugar. Add the cold water. Add the lemonade concentrate,
pineapple juice, and orange juice concentrate. Mix well and freeze.
Three hours before serving, remove from the freezer and allow it to
partially thaw. Mash it into a slushy consistency. Pour in the **Fresca®**.

Slush

6 ounces **Minute Maid®** orange juice concentrate
6 ounces **Minute Maid®** lemonade concentrate
2 1/2 cups water
1 cup sugar
1 can (15 1/2 ounces) pineapple tidbits
1 can (8 1/2 ounces) crushed pineapple
1 package (10 ounces) strawberries (or 2 pints fresh)
3 bananas, sliced

Mix the ingredients together in the order listed. Freeze the mixture in
quart containers. When ready to serve, let it thaw to a slushy
consistency. Serve in crystal compotes as an appetizer. Also makes

a great dessert. Leftovers can be refrozen. Children really like this for a great snack in the summer.

Easy Party Punch

2 packages unsweetened cherry Kool-Aid
1 gallon cold water
1 can (16 ounces) **Minute Maid®** orange juice concentrate
1 can (16 ounces) **Minute Maid®** lemonade concentrate
1 large can pineapple juice
1 quart **Fresca®**
2 cups sugar

Mix all of the ingredients well in a punch bowl. Enjoy.

Cold Punch

1 large can pineapple juice
1 large can **Minute Maid®** orange juice concentrate
1 bottle ReaLemon
2 cups sugar
1 cup water
2 quarts **Sprite®**

In a saucepan, boil the water and sugar until the mixture clears. Let cool.

Add all of the other ingredients and serve.

Bridal Punch

2 bottles (2 liter) **Fresca®**
6 bottles (2 liter) **Sprite®**
1 gallon lime sherbert
juice of 6 lemons
juice of 6 limes
2 large cans pineapple juice

Mix the lemon juice, lime juice, **Sprite®** and pineapple juice. When ready to serve, add the sherbert and **Fresca®**.

Green Wedding Punch

2 packages lime Jell-O
2 large cans pineapple juice
2 large bottles **Sprite®**
water

Completely dissolve the lime Jell-O in 2 cups of the pineapple juice. Add the remaining pineapple juice and **Sprite®** and enough water to make 2 gallons. Pour one gallon into ice trays or molds and freeze overnight. Store the other gallon in the refrigerator. Remove it from the mold and place in a cold punch bowl. Pour the other gallon over.

Red Fruit Punch

1 can (46 ounces) red fruit juice
1 large bottle **Fresca®**
1/2 gallon sherbert (raspberry or orange)

Mix the fruit juice and **Fresca®** together. Add the sherbert in chunks.

Pink Party Punch

1 tablespoon Crystal Light (fruit punch flavor)
1 large can pineapple juice
1 large bottle **Fresca®**

Mix all the ingredients together and place in gallon containers. Freeze. Let sit out for several hours and thaw to a slushy consistency. If necessary, cut off the top of the containers, to pour. Be sure the punch bowl is chilled before pouring in the punch.

Summertime Fruit Punch

3 cups **Minute Maid®** orange juice
1 1/2 cups fresh lemon juice, strained
1 bottle (48 ounces) cranberry juice cocktail
grated rind of 1 orange
grated rind of 1 lemon
2 cups water
2 cups sugar
2 teaspoons almond extract
1 quart **Fresca®**

In a medium saucepan, combine the orange and lemon rind, water, and sugar. Bring to a boil, and simmer for 5 minutes. Let cool. Stir in the almond extract and juices. Pour over ice and stir in **Fresca®**.

Sparkling Cranberry Punch

1 bottle (32 ounces) cranberry juice cocktail
1 can (6 ounces) **Minute Maid®** orange juice concentrate
1 can (6 ounces) **Minute Maid®** lemonade concentrate
2 cups water
ice ring or cubes
1 bottle (20 ounces) **Sprite®**, chilled
orange slices

Combine the fruit juices and water in a punch bowl. Just before serving, add ice. Holding the bottle on the rim of the bowl, carefully add the **Sprite®**. Garnish with orange slices.

Sparkling Cran-Grape Punch

2 quarts cranberry-grape juice, chilled
1 can (6 ounce) **Minute Maid®** pink lemonade concentrate
1 bottle (32 ounces) sparkling water, chilled

Mix the juice and lemonade concentrate in a punch bowl. Just before serving, stir in the sparkling water.

Cranberry Punch

3 cups sugar
1 gallon water
64 ounces cranberry juice
32 ounces apple juice
1 1/2 cups lemon juice
2 cups **Minute Maid®** orange juice
2 cups strong tea
2 quarts **Sprite®**

Bring the water and sugar to a boil and let cool. Mix with the fruit juices and tea. Chill. (If desired, a part of this recipe may be frozen into an ice ring, in order to not dilute the punch.) When ready to serve, add **Sprite®**.

Picnic Punch

1 can (46 ounces) red fruit juice, chilled
1 can (6 ounces) **Minute Maid®** lemonade concentrate
1 cup cranberry juice cocktail, chilled
ice cubes
orange slices

Combine the fruit juice, lemonade concentrate and cranberry juice and mix well. Add the ice cubes and orange slices.

Apple Sunshine Punch

4 cups unsweetened apple juice
2 cups pineapple juice, unsweetened
2 cups **Minute Maid®** orange juice
1/4 cup lemon juice

Combine all of the ingredients. Garnish with fresh mint, orange slices or cherries.

Tropical Coca-Cola® Punch

2/3 pint shredded pineapple
1/2 cup lemon juice
6 bottles (6 ounces) ice-cold **Coca-Cola®**
cracked ice
sprigs of mint

Combine the pineapple, lemon juice and **Coca-Cola®**. Put the cracked ice in a punch bowl and fill the bowl with the punch. Garnish with the sprigs of mint.

Coca-Cola® with Lemon Ice Cubes

1/2 cup lemon juice
1 quart of water
Coca-Cola®

Mix lemon juice and water. Fill ice cube trays and freeze. Use 3 to 4 cubes per bottle of **Coca-Cola®** and serve.

Coca-Cola® Lemon Cup

lemon juice
Coca-Cola®

Pour ice-cold **Coca-Cola®** into medium sized glasses and add 1 teaspoon of lemon juice for each bottle (6 ounce size) of **Coca-Cola®** used. For added zest, place the **Coca-Cola®** in the freezer just long enough to be half frozen, add a dash of lemon juice and serve.

Coca-Cola® Lime Cocktail

3 bottles (6 ounce size) **Coca-Cola®**
3 tablespoons of lime juice

Mix the lime juice and **Coca-Cola®**. Put in freezer for 45-60 minutes, stirring occasionally. Serve in slushy form in cocktail glasses. Garnish with mint.

Easy Punch

1/3 cup lime juice
1/2 cup **Minute Maid®** orange juice
1/2 cup sugar
1 liter **Fresca®**
ice cubes

Combine the lime juice and orange juice with the sugar. Stir until the sugar is dissolved. Add the **Fresca®** and serve over ice.

Coca-Cola® Orange Punch

1 cup sugar
1 cup hot fresh tea
1 pint cold water
1 cup **Minute Maid®** orange juice
1/2 cup lemon juice
5 bottles (6 ounce size) **Coca-Cola®**
thin slices of quartered orange

Dissolve the sugar in the hot tea and add the cold water. Let cool. Add the fruit juices. Pour over a large piece of ice in a punch bowl. Add the **Coca-Cola®** and orange slices.

Coca-Cola® with Orange Juice

Minute Maid® orange juice
Coca-Cola®

Add 1 tablespoon of orange juice to every 6 ounces of **Coca-Cola®**.

Red Party Punch

2 liters **cherry Coke®**
1 large can pineapple juice
1 liter **Sprite®**

Mix all the ingredients together. Makes two gallons.

Coca-Cola® Punch

grated rind of 6 lemons
2 1/4 cups fresh lemon juice
9 cups water
4 1/2 cups sugar
3 liters **Coca-Cola®**

Combine the lemon rind, juice, water and sugar, stirring until the sugar dissolves. Chill at least 4 hours or overnight. Stir in the **Coca-Cola®** just before serving. Serve over crushed ice.

Refreshing Mint Drink

2 cups sugar
1 cup water
2 handfuls fresh mint
juice of 6 lemons
Sprite®

In a saucepan, combine the sugar and water. Stir over medium heat until the mixture begins to clear. Remove from heat and add the fresh mint to the mixture. Let steam for 10 minutes. Strain the mixture. Add lemon juice. (May use fresh, reconstituted **Minute Maid®** or frozen) Refrigerate. Pour 1 1/2 small jiggers of the syrup (to taste) over ice cubes and add **Sprite®**. Makes a delicious, cool, refreshing drink. (May be used in iced tea.)

Hot Buttered Pineapple Drink

1 can (48 ounces) pineapple juice
2/3 cup **Minute Maid®** orange juice
2 tablespoons butter or margarine
2 teaspoons brown sugar
4 sticks (3 inches long) cinnamon

In a large saucepan, combine all of the ingredients and bring to a boil. Reduce the heat and simmer for 20 minutes. Remove the cinnamon sticks and serve hot.

Russian Tea

1 cup sugar
2 cups **Sprite®**
2 cups water
1 stick cinnamon
50 cloves
1 cup sugar
4 cups water
3 tea bags
1 large can pineapple juice
1 can (6 ounces) **Minute Maid®** orange juice concentrate

In a medium saucepan, simmer the first five ingredients for 20 minutes and set aside. In a separate pot, boil the next three ingredients and let stand for 5 minutes. Combine both mixtures along with the pineapple juice and orange juice. It is very sweet; the sugar content may be reduced to taste.

Zippy Red Eye

1 quart tomato juice
1 cup catsup
1 cup **Coca-Cola®**
2 tablespoons Worcestershire sauce
2 teaspoons hot sauce
1 teaspoon salt

Combine all of the ingredients and stir gently. Serve over ice.

Amber Tea Punch

4 cups hot tea
1/2 cup sugar
2 cans (12 ounces each) apricot nectar
2 cups **Minute Maid®** orange juice
1/2 cup lemon juice
28 ounces **Fresca®**, chilled
ice cubes

Combine the hot tea and sugar, stir until the sugar is dissolved. Stir in the nectar and juices. Chill.

Pour the mixture into a punch bowl, then carefully pour in the **Fresca®**. Serve over ice cubes.

Coke® Float

ice cream
Coca-Cola®

Fill a tall glass with vanilla, chocolate or butter pecan ice cream and pour **Coca-Cola®** over it.

Hawaiian Party Punch

1 can (46 ounces) unsweetened pineapple juice
2 bottles (32 ounces) **Fresca®**, chilled
3 quarts rainbow or raspberry sherbert

Combine all of the ingredients in a punch bowl.

Citrus Rhubarb Cooler

1 pound rhubarb, cut up (4 cups)
3 cups water
3/4 cup sugar
2/3 cup **Minute Maid®** orange juice
ice cubes
28 ounces **Fresca®**

In a saucepan, cook the rhubarb with the water and sugar for about 15 minutes or until the fruit is very soft. Press through a sieve. Add the fruit juice. Cover and chill. To serve, pour over ice cubes to half fill a tall glass. Finish filling the glass with **Fresca®**. Stir.

Mock Pink Champagne

> 1/2 cup sugar
> 1 cup water
> 1 cup grapefruit juice
> 1/2 cup **Minute Maid®** orange juice
> 1/4 cup grenadine syrup
> 28 ounces **Fresca®**, chilled
> twists of lemon peel
> maraschino cherries with stems on

Combine the sugar and water in a saucepan. Simmer uncovered, stirring constantly, until the sugar is dissolved, about 3 minutes, then cool.

Mix with the fruit juices and grenadine syrup in a punch bowl. Chill. Just before serving, add the **Fresca®**, pouring it slowly down the side of the bowl.

Serve over ice in sherbet glasses.

Trim each glass with the lemon peel and a cherry.

Grapefruit-Grenadine Punch

> 2 cans (46 ounces each) red fruit juice
> 2 cups grapefruit juice, chilled
> 1 cup grenadine syrup
> 2 cups **Sprite®**, chilled
> 1/2 orange, sliced (optional)
> 10 fresh strawberries (optional)

In a large punch bowl, combine the red fruit juice, grapefruit juice, and grenadine.

Just before serving, add the **Sprite®** and ice.

Garnish with orange slices and strawberries, if desired.

CHAPTER 14
MICROWAVE

I n a hurry? Do it the nineties way. Just throw that food into the microwave and nuke it. Quick meals don't have to taste bad, though. Not with the recipes that follow. Enjoy!

French Onion Soup

3 tablespoons butter or margarine
3 large onions, sliced
3 cups beef broth
1/2 cup water
1/2 cup **Coca-Cola®**
1 teaspoon Worcestershire sauce
salt and pepper, to taste
croutons
grated Parmesan cheese

In a 3 quart casserole dish, combine the butter and onions and cover with the lid. Cook at HIGH for 10 to 12 minutes, until the onions are tender. Stir in the broth, water, **Coca-Cola®**, Worcestershire, salt and pepper. Cook covered at HIGH for 10 minutes and at MEDIUM for 10 to 12 minutes. Let stand, covered, for 5 minutes before serving. Top individual servings with croutons and cheese.

Fish Fillets

2 small onions, sliced
2 tablespoons butter or margarine
1 clove garlic, finely chopped
1 can (16 ounces) stewed tomatoes, chopped
1 jar (4 1/2 ounces) sliced mushrooms, drained
1/4 cup **Sprite®**
1/8 teaspoon basil
6 flounder fillets (about 1/4 pound each)
salt

In a 12x8 inch dish, combine the onion, butter, and garlic. Cook, covered with plastic wrap, at HIGH for 3 to 3 1/2 minutes. Stir in the tomatoes, mushrooms, **Sprite®**, and basil. Cook, covered, at HIGH for 3 minutes and at MEDIUM for 3 to 4 minutes. While the vegetables are cooking, season the fish with salt on the skin side only and roll it up, skin side in. Arrange the rolls, seam side down, in the sauce and spoon the sauce over the fish. Cook, covered, at HIGH for 5 to 6 minutes, or until the fish is done. Let it stand, covered, for 5 minutes before serving.

Barbecued Chicken

1/2 cup catsup
1/2 cup **Coca-Cola®**
4 chicken breasts, boneless

Mix the catsup and **Coca-Cola®**. Place the chicken in a pan. Pour the sauce over the chicken. Cook, loosely covered with wax paper, on HIGH for 12 to 15 minutes. Rotate 1/2 turn after 6 minutes. Let stand, covered, for 2 to 3 minutes before serving.

Shepherd's Pie

2 cups cubed cooked turkey, chicken or beef
1 package (20 ounces) frozen broccoli,
    cauliflower, and carrot mix
1/4 cup frozen chopped onion
1 can (10 3/4 ounces) condensed cream of chicken soup

1/2 cup milk
1/4 cup **Coca-Cola**®
1/2 teaspoon leaf tarragon, crumbled
pepper to taste
frozen hash brown potatoes, cooked by package directions
or 2 cups mashed potatoes

In a 2 quart casserole dish, layer the meat with the frozen vegetable mix and onion. In a bowl, combine the soup, milk, **Coca-Cola**®, tarragon, and pepper, blending well. Pour over the vegetable layer. Arrange the potatoes evenly over the top. Microwave at HIGH for 10 to 15 minutes, until heated through.

Baked Beans

1 can pinto or red beans
6 ounces **Coca-Cola**®
diced onion to taste (approx 1/2 cup)
diced green pepper (approx 1/4 cup)
1/4 cup brown sugar
2 tablespoons mustard

Combine all the ingredients in a baking dish and cook on HIGH for 15 minutes, until bubbly.

Chocolate Pound Cake

1 package (18 1/2 ounce size) chocolate cake mix
1 package (4 1/2 ounce size) instant chocolate pudding mix
4 eggs
1 cup **Coca-Cola**®
1/4 cup oil

In a large bowl, combine all the ingredients. Beat at medium speed with an electric mixer for 4 minutes. Pour the batter into a greased 12 or 14 cup fluted tube dish. Cover with wax paper and cook at LOW for 10 minutes and at MEDIUM-HIGH for 6 to 7 minutes, until a toothpick inserted near the center comes out clean. Let it stand, uncovered, for 15 minutes before inverting on a serving platter. Let stand covered until cool.

An ad for **Coca-Cola®** from 1924,
when it sold for only 5 cents a glass.

CHAPTER 15
MISCELLANEOUS

Here are some recipes and other uses of **Coke®** that we couldn't figure out another place for. We think you'll find them of interest.

Give Your Car a Coke®

Here's something long used by wise old Southern taxi drivers (we first learned it from a cabbie in Columbus, Georgia in 1968). Next time you are driving through the pouring rain and have trouble seeing through the build up of road film on your windshield, try a **Coca-Cola®**. Splash some **Coke®** on the windshield and let the wipers spread it around. *Voila*, clean window! The rain will wash away any that spills on the body of the car. If you want to clean the other windows, you will need a paper towel.

Coca-Cola® Ice Cubes

Coca-Cola®

Pour **Coca-Cola®** into an ice cube tray and freeze. Use these ice cubes when serving **Coca-Cola®** in glasses. You can also freeze a maraschino cherry or mint cherry in the center of each cube to add interest.

Best Ever Granola

5 cups rolled oats
2 cups whole wheat flour
1 cup barley flour
1 cup rye flour
1 cup corn meal
1 cup pecan meal
1 cup wheat germ
1 cup coconut
1 cup brown sugar
1 tablespoon salt
1 cup oil
1/2 cup honey
1 cup **Sprite®**

Mix all of the ingredients in a large bowl. Spread on cookie sheets and bake at 250 to 275 degrees for 1 to 1-1/2 hours or until browned.

Chocolate Gravy

2 tablespoons cocoa
1/3 cup sugar
2 tablespoons flour
dash salt
1/4 cup **Coca-Cola®**
1 cup milk

In a saucepan, mix the cocoa, sugar, flour, and salt together until blended. Add the **Coca-Cola®** and cook over low heat until all the ingredients are dissolved. Add the milk and cook until the gravy boils and is thick. Good with biscuits, pancakes, or ice cream.

Apricot-Orange Conserve

3-1/2 cups apricots, chopped and drained (two 20 oz cans)
1-1/2 cups **Minute Maid®** orange juice
peel of 1/2 orange
2 tablespoons lemon juice
3-1/4 cups sugar
1/2 cup chopped nuts

In a saucepan, combine all of the ingredients, except the nuts. Cook until thick, stirring constantly. Add the nuts and stir well. Remove from the heat and skim. Fill and seal containers. Process for 5 minutes in a boiling water bath. Makes about 5 half-pint jars.

Index